D1473070

THIS BOOK PROPERTY OF
STANLEY J. BLAZEWSKI
519 W 2ND AV ROSSELLE NJ

The Naval Air War

NATHAN MILLER

The Naval Air War
1939-1945

Conway Maritime Press, Greenwich

THIS BOOK PROPERTY OF
STANLEY J. BLAZEWSKI
519 W 2ND AV ROSSELLE NJ

Copyright © 1980 by Nathan Miller. All rights reserved.
Published in the United Kingdom by Conway Maritime Press Ltd,
2 Nelson Road, Greenwich, London, SE10 9JB

ISBN 0 85177 201 3

All photographs are official U.S. Navy or furnished by
Popperfoto, London, U.K., unless otherwise indicated.

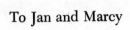

To Jan and Marcy

Books by Nathan Miller

The Naval Air War: 1939–1945
The Roosevelt Chronicles
The U.S. Navy: An Illustrated History
The Founding Finaglers: A History of Corruption in America
Sea of Glory: The Continental Navy Fights for Independence, 1775–1783

Contents

Preface

History records few stories more dramatic than that of naval aviation in World War II. At the outset of the conflict in 1939, it was regarded by some officers and strategists as a weapon of dubious quality and questionable utility. Nevertheless, naval aviation was to become a vital force in the Allied victory. Powerful, flexible and the most mobile of all weapons used at sea, naval air power had a decisive influence upon events in all theatres of operation. The airplane and the aircraft carrier inspired new tactics and technologies, resulting in a revolution in naval warfare as profound as that caused by the introduction of steam and armor plate. For the first time, naval battles were fought without the opposing fleets ever catching sight of each other.

The naval air war had three distinct stages, each of increasing complexity. In the first phase, which lasted from the outbreak of the war until the Japanese attack on Pearl Harbor, the carrier and its aircraft were subordinate to the battleship. Their primary tasks were to protect the battle fleet from attack, to serve as its eyes and as an extension of its big guns. The *Bismarck* episode and the Battle of Matapan, in which the Royal Navy used its air arm to cripple enemy fighting ships so that they could be brought under the guns of the battle fleet, were the highpoints of this era. The devastating attack by British torpedo planes on the Italian fleet as it lay at anchor in Taranto harbor represented a shift of tactics —foreshadowing the bold use of Japanese naval air power at Pearl Harbor.

In the second phase, the U.S. Navy, deprived of its battleships by the successful Japanese attack on its Hawaiian base, was forced to rely upon its handful of carriers to strike back. Fortunately, there had been experiments with such operations during the fleet exercises of the 1930s, and there was a foundation of experience upon which to build. The carrier replaced the battleship through necessity, and fleet operations were subordinated to the carrier's requirements. The decisive battles of the Coral Sea and Midway, along with the other air-sea battles of the middle years of the war, were fought with this imperative in mind.

The third phase of the naval air war followed the Battle of the Philippine Sea in June 1944. After destroying the Japanese fleet and its air units, the Fast Carrier Task Force controlled the skies over Japan. Along with the blockade of the home islands established by American submarines and the B-29 fire raids on Japanese cities, carrier-borne strikes helped to bring Japan to its knees. Not only had the Fast Carrier Task Force superseded the battleship, but it had become the instrument through which the U.S. Navy projected its power over land and sea alike.

Despite its importance, the story of naval aviation in World War II has largely been neglected. Furthermore, most of the books that deal in detail with air operations are devoted almost entirely to the Pacific theatre, with no mention made of developments in the Atlantic and Mediterranean. This book is intended as an account of the sea-air war in which operations in all theatres, by both the Allies and Axis, are treated in a balanced fashion. Particular emphasis has also been placed upon the men who fought this war and their personal triumphs and tragedies. Inevitably in a book of limited size, however, accounts of some operations have had to be truncated or slighted but I have tried to present as unbiased and reasonably complete account of the naval air war from 1939 to 1945 as possible within the space allowed.

I wish to express my thanks to Judy Spahr, who typed the manuscript; David Hall of Popperfoto in London and Edward Hine of the Imperial War Museum, both of whom went beyond normal courtesy in assisting a visiting American in his picture research; Agnes F. Hoover and Charles R. Haberlein of the Photographic Section of the U.S. Naval Historical Division, who were generous with their time and knowledge; and to Robert W. Love, Jr., Assistant Professor of History at the U.S. Naval Academy who wrote the picture captions. I am indebted to Kenneth J. Hagan, Associate

Professor of History at the Naval Academy, who read the book in manuscript and suggested many improvements. My wife, Jeanette, sustained me with her patience and understanding.

NATHAN MILLER

Chevy Chase, Maryland

History is the one sure guide to the future—that and imagination.

—*Winston S. Churchill*

1

Day of Fury

0600 hours, Sunday, December 7, 1941.

Bows flinging off white clouds of spray, six aircraft carriers flying the sunburst flag of Japan turned into the wind to launch their deadly brood. As Commander Mitsuo Fuchida's plane roared down the pitching deck of the flagship *Akagi* into the dawning sky, the crew sped him on his way with three ceremonial *Banzais*. Within fifteen minutes, 183 aircraft—Kate torpedo and high-level bombers, Val dive bombers and Zero fighters—were headed south toward Pearl Harbor, main base of the U.S. Pacific Fleet on the Hawaiian island of Oahu, about 230 miles away. Japan had chosen to wage war with the United States—and the most powerful concentration of naval air power yet seen was speeding on its way to battle.

War had long been brewing in the Pacific. Bogged down with their war in China, the Japanese desperately needed the oil and other resources of Southeast Asia and the Dutch East Indies to keep their military machine running. The summer of 1941 had seemed a good time to seize these areas. The war had been underway in Europe for more than two years and a beleaguered Britain was struggling to maintain control of the Suez Canal; France had been defeated; Russia was reeling under a savage German onslaught and American eyes were fixed on the momentous events unfolding across the Atlantic. In fact, the U.S. Navy was already engaged in an undeclared war with German U-boats. The Japanese began their march to the south by occupying French Indochina in July 1941. Long suspicious of what it regarded as Japan's aggressive ambitions, the United States demanded an immediate withdrawal. When this ultimatum was ignored, Washington tightened an embargo on the shipment of oil and other materiel to

3

Japan. The Japanese military, which had seized control of the government, resolved to answer the American threat with war.

As strategists have done throughout history, the Japanese tended to prepare for the next war in terms of the previous one. In case of a conflict with the United States, they had planned to use their fleet to capture the Philippines, strike for the East Indies, and then confront the advancing Americans in a climactic sea battle in the Central Pacific. But Admiral Isoroku Yamamoto, Commander-in-Chief of the Combined Fleet, conceived a much more daring plan. Having seen America's industrial might at first hand as a naval attaché in Washington, he declared that Japan had no hope of winning a war with the United States "unless the U.S. Fleet in Hawaiian waters can be destroyed."[1]

Yamamoto urged that a surprise carrier strike be made against the American battleships and carriers as they lay at anchor at Pearl Harbor. Such a move would take full advantage of Japan's temporarily superior naval power in the Pacific—ten battleships to nine, and ten carriers to three. There was ample precedent for such an assault. Japan had launched wars against Russia and China with massive surprise attacks. And during the U.S. Navy's fleet exercises of 1932, Admiral Harry E. Yarnell had successfully "raided" Pearl Harbor one quiet Sunday morning. Overcoming considerable opposition, Yamamoto argued that with the American fleet out of action, Japan would be able to conquer the Philippines, Singapore and the East Indies without interference. It could then retire behind a strong defense line running from the Kuriles to the fringes of Malaya. Using interior lines of communication and supply, the Imperial Navy would be able to beat off all attacks on this barrier. The Western allies would become weary of fighting a two-ocean war while suffering heavy losses, and would be forced to accept Japan's domination of the "Greater East Asia Co-Prosperity Sphere."

A diplomatic ballet designed to mask Japanese intentions unfolded in Tokyo and Washington, as preparations were made for the attack on Pearl Harbor. The Japanese Navy's most experienced pilots and air crews were assigned to Plan Z—as the Pearl Harbor operation was known—and technicians were put to work developing improved armor-piercing bombs and torpedoes that would run true in the shallow waters of Pearl Harbor. Every pilot had

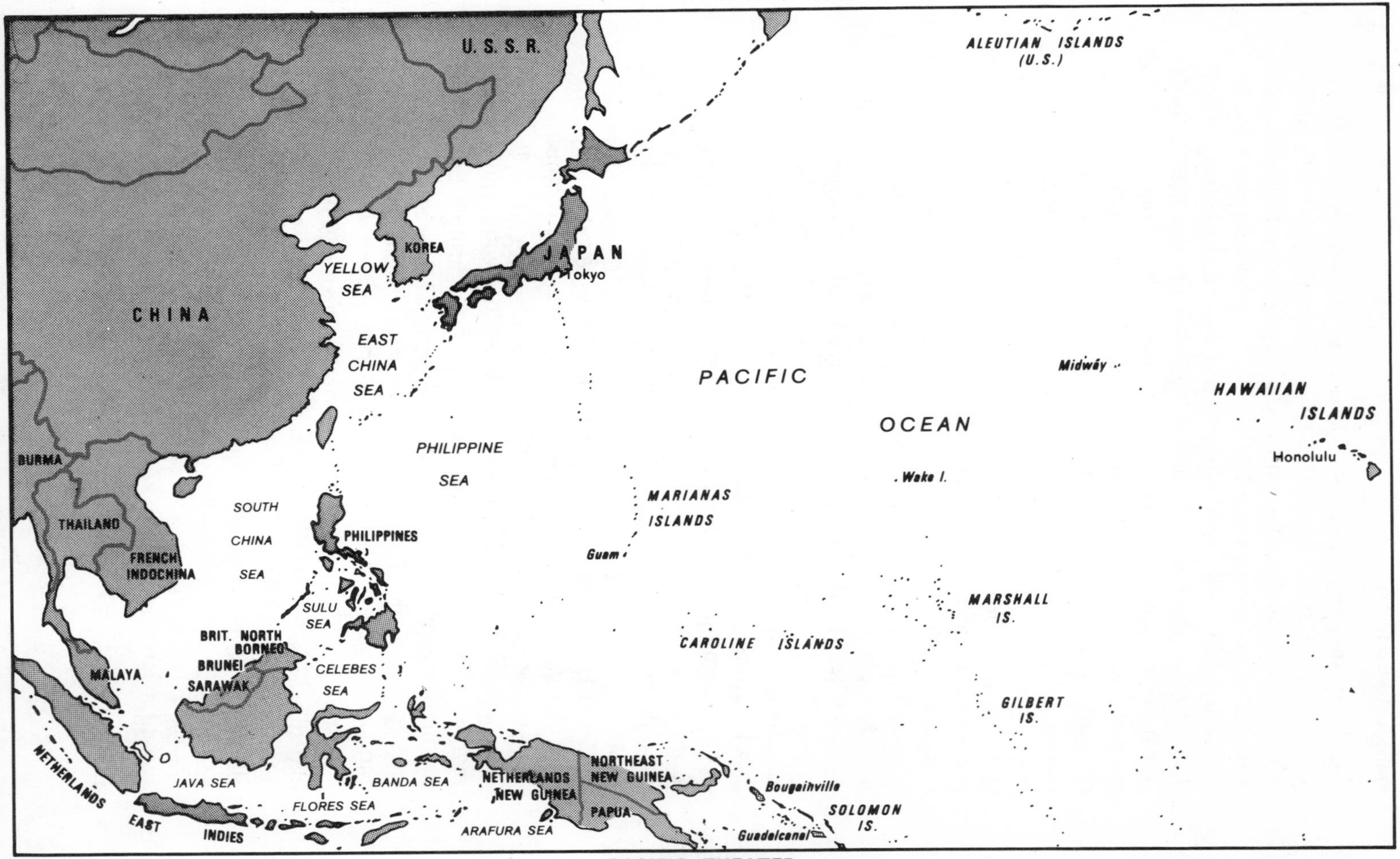

ALEUTIAN ISLANDS
(U.S.)

HAWAIIAN ISLANDS

Honolulu

U.S.S.R.

JAPAN
Tokyo

Midway

KOREA

YELLOW SEA

EAST CHINA SEA

CHINA

PACIFIC OCEAN

Wake I.

MARSHALL IS.

GILBERT IS.

PHILIPPINE SEA

MARIANAS ISLANDS

Guam

CAROLINE ISLANDS

SOLOMON IS.

Bougainville

Guadalcanal

SOUTH CHINA SEA

PHILIPPINES

SULU SEA

CELEBES SEA

BRIT. NORTH BORNEO

BRUNEI

SARAWAK

BANDA SEA

NETHERLANDS NEW GUINEA

NORTHEAST NEW GUINEA

PAPUA

ARAFURA SEA

FLORES SEA

JAVA SEA

BURMA

THAILAND

FRENCH INDOCHINA

MALAYA

NETHERLANDS EAST INDIES

PACIFIC THEATER

his designated target and had been trained to hit it. Finally, on November 26, 1941, the carriers of the First Air Fleet—the *Akagi*, *Hiryu*, *Soryu*, *Kaga*, *Shokaku*, and *Zuikaku*—crammed with 425 planes and guarded by two battleships and other escorts under the command of Vice Admiral Chuichi Nagumo, disappeared into the thick fog of the North Pacific. Meanwhile, ominous reports of Japanese troop movements along the coast of Southeast Asia were picked up by American intelligence, and on November 27, Washington sent a "war warning" to Admiral Husband E. Kimmel, commander of the Pacific Fleet at Pearl Harbor, informing him of an expected attack on the Philippines, Thailand or Borneo. Believing Hawaii to be in no imminent danger, Kimmel did not order his fleet on full alert, rig anti-torpedo nets, raise barrage balloons or disperse his aircraft.

Undetected, the Japanese planes droned in on Oahu, as the clouds broke and the sun slanted down on an empty sea. Shortly before 0700, the destroyer *Ward* reported making a contact with an unidentified submarine near the entrance to Pearl Harbor, and depth-charged it. The report was delayed in transit to Kimmel's headquarters. Not long afterward, two Army radar operators at the northern tip of Oahu picked up a swarm of aircraft closing fast from the northeast. Without checking, their superiors took this to be a flight of B-17 Flying Fortresses expected in from the West Coast.

"Pearl Harbor was still asleep in the morning mist," one of the Japanese pilots later reported. "It was calm and serene inside the harbor, not even a trace of smoke arising from the ships at Oahu. The orderly groups of barracks, the wiggling white line of automobiles climbing up the mountaintop; fine objectives of attack lay in all directions."[2] Seven battleships were moored with awnings spread on Battleship Row on the east side of Ford Island in the middle of the harbor and the flagship *Pennsylvania* was in drydock. Luckily for the Americans, none of their three carriers were in port. The *Saratoga* was undergoing repairs on the West Coast and the *Lexington* and *Enterprise* were ferrying planes to the Marine garrisons at Wake and Midway Islands.

The ships were just coming to life. Many of the officers and enlisted men were enjoying weekend liberty ashore, and others were having a late breakfast. The Honolulu radio station was broadcasting light music and the sound of church bells drifted across the gently rippling waters. At 0755, as parties began to form for the traditional raising of the colors, some of the men idly noted a line of aircraft sweeping in over the green mountains to the north of the base. Suddenly the planes swooped down on the air station on Ford Island, and the Sunday morning peace was ripped apart by the sound of bomb explosions.

The airfields scattered about the island—Hickam, Wheeler, Ewa,

Admiral Isoroku Yamamoto, Commander-in-Chief of the Japanese Combined Fleet.

and Kaneohe—were the first targets of the Japanese fighters and dive bombers. Some of the bombers plunged to within a few hundred feet of the ground before releasing, to ensure the highest accuracy. Lined up wing-to-wing as if for inspection—it was easier to guard them from sabotage that way—dozens of Army, Navy and Marine planes were blasted into twisted and burning piles of scrap metal. Only a few of the defenders were able to get into the air and most were quickly shot down by the highly maneuverable Zeros. Ground crews and pilots tried to fight back with machine guns wrenched from the wrecked planes, but to little avail. Within minutes the Japanese had completely knocked out Oahu's air defenses. Observing the devastation from one of the high-level bombers, Commander Fuchida flashed a coded signal back to Admiral Nagumo on the *Akagi*: "Tora . . . Tora . . . Tora" (Tiger . . . Tiger . . . Tiger) which meant that the surprise attack had succeeded.

Sweeping in from several directions at little more than forty feet above the water, the Kates dropped their torpedoes with deadly precision. Chief Flight Petty Officer Juzo Mori suddenly found a battleship looming up "directly in front of my speeding plane; it towered ahead of the bomber like a great mountain peak." Oblivious to the intense antiaircraft fire, he continued to bore in. "Prepare for release . . . Stand by . . . Release torpedo!" Mori jerked with all his might at the torpedo release and felt his plane pitch upward as it was freed of its burden. With defensive fire growing heavier every second, he turned away and headed south for the open sea. "I was so frightened," he said, "that before I left the target area my clothes were soaking with perspiration."[3]

Every one of the outboard ships on Battleship Row was hit several times by torpedoes, and Pearl Harbor was dotted with towering waterspouts. Dark gray puffs of antiaircraft fire exploded about Fuchida's plane as he led his bombers over the battleships to complete the task of destruction. He felt his craft "bounce as if struck by a club, but it was not hit. On his bombing run, he observed the fall of the bombs through a hole in the plane's floor. "I watched four bombs plummet toward the earth. The target—two battleships moored side by side—lay ahead. The bombs became smaller and smaller and finally disappeared. I held my breath

The Pearl Harbor raid was meant to knock out the U.S. Pacific Fleet long enough to enable the Japanese to establish their empire, and build a firm line of defense across the central Pacific. Here we see a photograph taken from a Japanese aircraft, early in the attack. In the foreground is Battleship Row; the *West Virginia*, in the center foreground on the outboard side, is about to be struck by a Japanese torpedo, whose wake can be clearly seen. In the background, Hickam Field burns from the intense bombardment.

until two tiny puffs of smoke flashed suddenly on the ship to the left, and I shouted, 'Two hits!' "[4]

Fuchida's aircraft was rocked by the force of a tremendous explosion as the battleship *Arizona* blew up. An armor-piercing bomb had smashed through the steel deck of the *Arizona*, which had already been hit by a torpedo. The bomb then touched off a forward magazine. Huge pieces of the vessel were hurled hundreds of feet into the air and a dark red cloud of smoke billowed into the sky. Torn in half and swept by towering flames, the *Arizona* became a deadly inferno for nearly 1,100 officers and men.

The *West Virginia* was struck by six or seven torpedoes that ripped a gash 120 feet long and 15 feet wide in her port side, and

9

An aerial view of Pearl Harbor shows the drydock area and damage done by the Japanese attack on December 7, 1941. The battleship *Pennsylvania* is in the lower drydock area, with the burned-out destroyers *Cassin* and *Downes* ahead of her. Despite the fact that she was in the drydock, the *Pennsylvania* was prepared for the attack, and later claimed six enemy aircraft were downed by her antiaircraft fire.

keeled over into the mud. The *Oklahoma,* hit by a spread of three torpedoes, rolled over. Two torpedoes hit the *California* and only counter-flooding prevented the vessel from capsizing. The *Maryland, Tennessee* and *Pennsylvania* escaped serious damage but were unable to get to sea because the first two vessels were wedged in by sinking ships and the *Pennsylvania* was in drydock. Only the *Nevada,* which had steam up in two of her boilers at the time of the attack, managed to get underway, despite heavy bow damage from a torpedo.

At 0854, a second wave of 170 Japanese planes continued the onslaught against the airfields and ships, now almost hidden by billowing clouds of black, oily smoke. Flight after flight of dive bombers attacked the *Nevada,* which had backed out of the flaming oil spewing from the *Arizona's* blasted hulk. The Japanese planes tried to sink her at the narrow entrance to Pearl Harbor. Although a shambles topside, she survived by throwing up a heavy curtain of antiaircraft fire. But she took on water too rapidly to maintain steerageway, and was finally beached off Hospital Point. Eighteen SBD dive bombers from the returning *Enterprise* and the dozen Flying Fortresses expected from the mainland were unlucky enough to arrive midway in the Japanese attack, and were pounced upon by the Zeros. Several of them were shot down before they had a chance to defend themselves. Others fell victim to the antiaircraft gunners who were firing at anything in the air. "Please don't shoot! Don't shoot!" cried one pilot. "This is an American plane!" And then his radio went dead.

For nearly two hours, until about 0945, the Japanese dominated

The first wave of Japanese attackers struck the combat aircraft lined up on the field of the Naval Air Station on Ford Island in Pearl Harbor. At least 177 American planes were lost completely, and as many damaged. There was no effective air opposition during the remainder of the Japanese assault on the Pacific Fleet. Nonetheless, these losses were trifling: in 1943, American aerospace firms built over 100,000 military aircraft—and still had excess capacity!

A motor launch rescues a survivor from the waters of Pearl Harbor, as the battleship *West Virginia*, ravaged by Japanese torpedoes, burns in the background. She would later sink at her berth. Beyond her is the *Tennessee*, which was also damaged in the attack.

the skies over Pearl Harbor, strafing and bombing targets at will. In all, 353 planes participated in the attack. By the time they returned to their carriers, the oil-coated anchorage was dotted with the wreckage of nineteen ships, including almost the entire battle line of the Pacific Fleet. An estimated 265 aircraft of all types had also been destroyed, leaving only a handful still operational. American casualties totaled 2,403 dead and 1,178 wounded; the Japanese lost 29 planes and 55 airmen.

Upon his return to the *Akagi*, the elated Fuchida pressed Admiral Nagumo for another strike against the repair shops and fuel storage tanks at Pearl Harbor, and suggested a search be launched for the *Enterprise* and *Lexington* which were thought to be somewhere south of Oahu. Nagumo refused, pointing out that a rendezvous had already been planned with tankers, and if the task force was delayed it would be short of fuel. So orders were given to turn to the northward and the Japanese slipped away as swiftly and silently as they had come.

Japanese naval air power had inflicted on the U.S. Navy its most humiliating defeat ever. As President Franklin D. Roosevelt said, December 7, 1941 is "a date which will live in infamy" for Americans. Nevertheless, the Japanese had won only a temporary victory. Except for the *Arizona,* all the stricken battleships were raised from the mud of Pearl Harbor, and all but the *Oklahoma* would see action. The attackers erred in neglecting the American oil tanks and machine shops. Most damaging, though, was the failure of the Japanese to knock out the American aircraft carriers. Unable to rely on their battleships in the early part of the war, the Americans were forced to resort to the carrier as the principal naval weapon of the war in the Pacific—and the fast carrier task force became the spearhead of the U.S. Navy's victorious offensive against Japan.

The *California* settles on the bottom of Pearl Harbor. Raised, repaired, and modernized, the twelve 14-inch guns of the *California* were installed on other battleships. In October 1944 during the Battle of Leyte Gulf, a Japanese surface squadron tried to force a passage through Surigao Strait, where it was massacred by American firepower—including the guns from the old *California!*

2

A Band of Brothers____

Fifteen years before the outbreak of World War II, Admiral William S. Sims, president of the U.S. Naval War College, foresaw with remarkable clarity the manner in which the sea battles of the future would be fought. "A fleet whose carriers give it command of the air over the enemy fleet can defeat the latter," he said. "The fast carrier is the capital ship of the future."[5] Yet when war came on September 3, 1939, naval aviation was regarded with mistrust and suspicion by traditionalists who believed in the supremacy of the battleship and the big gun. They regarded the airplane as a weapon of dubious reliability, suitable only for scouting and patrol work. Should airplanes attempt to bomb or torpedo battleships, according to the conventional wisdom, they would be immediately shot out of the sky by the antiaircraft guns of the ships.

Britain's Royal Navy had pioneered in the use of aircraft at sea during World War I, launching the first carrier-borne strike against an enemy target on July 19, 1918. Four of the six Sopwith Camels which bombed the Zeppelin sheds at Tondern on the North Sea failed to return to the carrier *Furious*, but this was considered a small price to pay for the fiery destruction of two Zeppelins which were being used to bomb London. Before the Armistice, however, the Royal Navy lost control of its air units to the newly organized Royal Air Force, which was given responsibility for both land- and sea-based aircraft. To this shotgun wedding the navy brought a dowry of some 2,500 planes and 55,000 men. It was not to regain control of seaborne aviation again for two decades—a period in which the Fleet Air Arm, Britain's naval air service, declined relative to the air units of the American and Japanese navies, which had retained control of their planes.

15

In the battle for a fair share of the limited defense funds available during the 1920s and 30s, the Royal Navy came off poorly. The handful of aircraft it received were not designed for use at sea but were mostly converted land-based aircraft and were grossly inferior to those being flown from American and Japanese carriers. When Britain declared war on Nazi Germany, the Fleet Air Arm had seven carriers, 232 operational planes and only 700 pilots and aircrewmen. With the exception of the 23,000-ton *Ark Royal* which carried 60 planes, the carriers were all aging veterans. Most of the aircraft were outmoded canvas-covered biplanes—rickety Swordfish torpedo planes that had first taken to the air in 1931, Sea Gladiator fighters, and cumbersome Walrus seaplanes. The only relatively modern plane was the Skua, a two-place monoplane designated as both a fighter and dive bomber. While it was an excellent dive bomber, it was slower than the German bombers it was supposed to shoot down.

But the pilots, observers and gunners of the Fleet Air Arm were uniformly outstanding. Through years of adversity, they had become like a band of brothers. With energy, enthusiasm and a proud faith in the decisive role of naval air power in any war to come, they made the best use of their limited resources and obsolescent planes. And when war came, they became legendary for their unflagging courage in the face of demoralizing odds—in Arctic waters, in the North Atlantic, in the Mediterranean, and in the Pacific.

Luckily for the British, the Germans had also neglected their naval air units. Hermann Goering, Chief of the Luftwaffe (the German air force) controlled all air operations, declaring that "anything that flies belongs to me," but the sea was a foreign element to him. An aircraft carrier, the *Graf Zeppelin*, had been laid down but she was never completed. In 1942, plans were discussed to convert the liners *Europa* and *Potsdam* to auxiliary carriers, the former to carry forty-two planes and the latter twenty, but the proposal was scrapped because Germany did not have aircraft suitable for carrier operations.

The early months of World War II were anything but a "phony war" for the Fleet Air Arm. It immediately went on the offensive against the German submarines lying athwart the shipping lanes to Britain. The Admiralty established two antisubmarine hunter-

Displacing 23,000 tons and carrying seventy aircraft, the *Ark Royal* was the largest of the British wartime carriers. She lacked the extensive armor protection, radar and improved antiaircraft guns which were introduced in the *Illustrious* class. But the *Ark Royal* nonetheless served with great distinction and was repeatedly "sunk" by German propaganda before she actually fell victim to a U-boat.

killer groups built around the carriers *Ark Royal* and *Courageous*. These vessels were ill-equipped for the task assigned them. Captain S. W. Roskill, official historian of the Royal Navy's operations in World War II, has traced the decision to risk them thus to pressure from Winston Churchill, then First Lord of the Admiralty, to go on the offensive "rather than to devote our maximum effort to the defensive strategy of convoy and escort."[6] But it was not long before the hunters became the hunted. On September 14, the *Ark Royal* was operating west of the Hebrides when the *U-39* fired a salvo of torpedoes at her. Only the premature explosion of the torpedoes, due to their defective detonators, saved the carrier. The escorting destroyers promptly launched a counterattack, sinking the submarine and capturing her crew.

Three days later, the 22,500-ton *Courageous* was not so lucky. The *U-29* was trying to intercept a convoy reported by another

17

A modification of the famous Spitfire, the Seafire provided the high-performance combat air cover for British aircraft carriers that they had lacked early in the war. However, the Seafire's narrow undercarriage and high landing speed gave it poor handling characteristics which caused a number of accidents. In addition, its wings did not fold; this feature limited the number that could be taken aboard the small British carriers. It reflected a longstanding British policy of attempting, with limited success, to achieve "commonality" between land-based and seaborne aircraft.

submarine in the Western Approaches when she sighted the carrier some distance away. The U-boat's skipper despaired of making an attack until the *Courageous* unexpectedly slowed to recover some of her forty-eight aircraft, while all but two of the screening destroyers were dispatched to assist a merchant vessel that had been attacked. Exploiting their luck to the full, the Germans crept to within 3,000 yards of the target without being detected, and fired three torpedoes at the carrier. Two of them struck the *Courageous* and she sank within fifteen minutes, taking 518 of her officers and men with her. Surviving a depth charge attack by the escort, the *U-29* returned safely to its base, having scored the war's first notable naval victory. The sinking of the *Courageous* finally convinced the Admiralty that carriers were unsuited for antisubmarine warfare.

Worried about the depredations of German surface raiders, the British organized several hunter groups built around the five remaining carriers. Fanning out over the sea, they searched some six million square miles of ocean during the early months of the war. The only unit to see action was Force K, built around the *Ark Royal*. Leading a sortie into the North Sea on September 25, 1939, her Skuas shot down a Dornier 18 which was shadowing the squadron—the first German aircraft of the war to be destroyed by a British plane.

Taking off and landing in all kinds of weather, performing long-range searches and conducting operations far from their bases, the air crews improved their skills, even though they made no contact with their quarry. The mere presence at sea of the carriers was an effective weapon, however, for German commanders did not know when planes might drop out of the sky on them. In fact, a skillful British game of bluff convinced Captain Hans Langsdorff of the powerful *Admiral Graf Spee* that the *Ark Royal* lay in wait for him at the mouth of the River Plate. This deception played a large part in Langsdorff's decision to scuttle the ship. The carrier was actually 2,000 miles away.

The attention of both Germany and Britain was focused on the rugged coastline of Norway during the early spring of 1940. To avoid capture by the Royal Navy, blockade runners, carrying the Swedish iron ore which was vital to the German war effort, hugged the Norwegian coast, in violation of Norway's neutrality. The British planned to mine these waters and thus force the enemy vessels out into the open sea. Alarmed, the Germans struck first. On April 9, 1940, they launched a daring invasion of Norway, despite the Royal Navy's command of the sea. Norwegian resistance was weak and the invaders quickly established themselves at Narvik, Bergen, Oslo, Trondheim and other key points. A sizeable British task force, including the *Furious,* was dispatched to interrupt the invasion, but the carrier put to sea so hurriedly that she sailed without embarking her fighter squadron—making her all but useless in the ensuing operations.

The Royal Navy quickly learned the cost of bringing its ships within range of land-based bombers without fighter cover. For three hours, nearly ninety German bombers lashed at the squadron as it steamed off the Norwegian coast, damaging the battleship *Rodney* and three cruisers, and sinking a destroyer. The Germans scored not only a tactical but a strategic victory, because the British ships had to move out of the range of the German bombers and were unable to attack the invasion force or interfere with German sea communications with Norway.

The British struck back the following day. Sixteen Skuas took off from Hatston in the Orkneys in the early morning darkness of April 10 bound for Bergen, three hundred miles away, where the German cruiser *Königsberg* lay anchored. Each carrying a 500-pound bomb and a full load of fuel, the planes lumbered into the air, some of them barely managing to clear the runway. Two hours later they crossed the rugged Norwegian coastline as the sun was coming up, and climbed to 8,000 feet. On reaching Bergen, the

A British Seafire IIC makes a flapless take-off in light wind conditions. It had a speed of 342 mph and was armed with eight machine guns or two to four 20-mm cannon, but its usefulness was hampered by a short operating range.

Skuas screamed down on the surprised Germans, and smothered the *Königsberg* in direct hits and near misses. Turned into a blazing wreck, she exploded and sank at her mooring, the war's first dive-bombing victim. Flying low through heavy antiaircraft fire, the British planes zig-zagged down Bergen Fjord, all but one making good their escape. The margin of safety was so fine, however, that upon landing at Hatston, the engines of several of the aircraft sputtered and died before they taxied off the runway. They had run out of fuel. Ironically, a BBC radio broadcast that night credited the Fleet Air Arm's most spectacular accomplishment of the campaign to the R.A.F.—whose bombers had failed to find the *Königsberg* the day before.

At about the same time that this attack was taking place, a British destroyer flotilla had fought its way into the harbor of Narvik, sinking two German destroyers and damaging three others. Five enemy destroyers were undamaged and on April 13, the battleship *Warspite* and the *Furious* were assigned the task of destroying them. The carrier's Swordfish, along with a Swordfish catapulted off the *Warspite*, searched out targets for the battleship's 15-inch guns. The *Warspite* pummeled and destroyed one of the vessels, while the Swordfish bombed and sank a U-boat found lurking in the fjord.

For the British, these were the last true successes of the frustrating battle for Norway. They were never able to overcome the initial advantage of surprise won by the Germans and their countermeasures were ill-planned, lacking clear-cut objectives. Because the R.A.F. lacked planes with the range to reach Norway from its bases in Britain, the Fleet Air Arm was required to do battle with a first-rate, land-based air force—something it was never designed to do. Time after time, pilots and air crews were called upon to sacrifice themselves for a lost cause in obsolete planes completely unsuited to the missions assigned them. Poor flying conditions, sudden snow squalls, and mountains that suddenly appeared out of the mists all made the campaign an airman's nightmare. Before it was over, Fleet Air Arm casualties would amount to almost a third of the organization's total flying strength.

Nevertheless, Britain pressed on with the battle for Norway. The *Ark Royal* and the *Glorious* arrived off Trondheim on April 23 and launched their Skuas in support of a British landing. Fearing

A Swordfish torpedo bomber from the British escort carrier *Archer*, one of the first of this type to be converted from a merchant hull. The aircraft, a anachronism which had a top speed of 138 mph, nevertheless achieved extraordinary success in the early years of the conflict against German and Italian warships. Nicknamed the "stringbag," she had a range of 546 miles, carried a three-man crew, was armed with two "303" Vickers machine guns, and could drop one 1,600-pound torpedo.

The Blackburn Skua was the Fleet Air Arm's first modern aircraft, and was used as both a fighter and dive bomber.

German air attacks, the ships remained about 100 miles from the coast, a situation which placed their aircraft at a disadvantage. When the British pilots tried to break up a bombing raid by Junkers 88s on the beachheads, they found their planes too slow to catch the German aircraft. Then, starting to run short of fuel, the Skuas set a course for the carrier—but before they could land, three of them ran out of gas and crashed. Twenty-six Swordfish and ten Skuas attacked the Germans the following morning, destroying three enemy aircraft and damaging three supply ships. But four planes were shot down and another seven were lost after running out of fuel. The British pilots were also chagrined to find that their torpedoes exploded short of their targets in the shallow waters of the Norwegian fjords.

One of the *Ark Royal*'s Skua pilots, Major Richard T. Partridge of the Royal Marines, who had taken part in the *Königsberg* raid, shot down a German bomber in one of these sweeps, and then was shot down himself. He crash-landed on a frozen lake, and he and his observer struggled through deep snow to a nearby cabin. The British airmen had just settled down when the crew of the German bomber they had shot down came through the door. An uneasy truce prevailed through the night. At dawn, they were all arrested by a Norwegian ski patrol which eventually provided the Englishmen with skis and a map showing the route to the coast. "We made a very comprehensive tour of a large portion of Norway on foot, by car and by boat," Partridge commented dryly upon his return to the *Ark Royal*. "We both agreed it was a very lovely country."[7]

The fighting shifted north to Narvik where the British put another expedition ashore. Eighteen R.A.F. Gladiators were flown off the *Glorious* and, operating from a frozen lake, they quickly shot down six enemy aircraft. But not long afterward, they were caught on the ground and most of them were destroyed. This again placed the brunt of the air war in the hands of the Fleet Air Arm. Walruses and Swordfish faced enemy aircraft with three times their speed and six times their firepower. A Walrus even managed to shoot down a Junkers 88. "Delayed by three Heinkels," signaled a laconic Swordfish pilot who somehow managed to escape. One patrol ended when a Swordfish and two Gladiators were caught in a blinding snowstorm and crashed into a mountain.

23

A Martlet, the British designation for American F4F fighters transferred to the Admiralty under the Lend-Lease Act, taxis aboard the *Illustrious* in March 1942. About nine hundred of these planes were delivered during the war.

Following the German breakthrough on the Western Front, the ill-starred Norwegian campaign was brought to an end. The remaining R.A.F. Gladiators and a handful of Hurricanes that had joined them returned to the *Glorious* for evacuation. Although the pilots had never made deck landings before and the planes were not fitted with arresting gear, they landed safely. The *Glorious* headed for the naval base at Scapa Flow, escorted by a pair of destroyers, when on June 8 she ran afoul of the German battle-cruisers *Gneisenau* and *Scharnhorst*. For some reason no defensive patrols were being flown by her planes, and a last-minute attempt to launch torpedo-carrying Swordfish came too late. The German vessels' 11-inch guns made short work of the luckless carrier. The two destroyers were also sunk, but not before one of them, the *Acasta*, put a torpedo into the *Scharnhorst*, seriously damaging her. Of the 1,561 sailors and airmen in the three ships, only 46 survived the cold waters of the Arctic Sea.

The *Scharnhorst* limped into Trondheim, and on June 13 the *Ark Royal* sent sixteen Skuas to avenge the sinking of the *Glorious*. The mission exemplified the failures of the hapless Norwegian campaign. Clear weather eliminated any chance of surprise and the flak was heavy. Even before the dive bombers could begin their attack they were set upon by swarms of Messerschmitt fighters which completely outclassed them. The only bomb to strike the battlecruiser turned out to be a dud. Eight British planes were lost. Among those shot down was Major Partridge. Although badly burned, he survived five years as a prisoner of war. A week later, while the *Scharnhorst* was returning to Kiel for repairs, she was unsuccessfully attacked by a half-dozen Swordfish, two of which were shot down.

So ended the Norwegian tragedy. The only bright aspect of the campaign was the bravery of those who did the fighting—and dying. "The unswerving constancy of purpose of the young men who bore the brunt of the sea and air fighting during these unhappy weeks shines in strong contrast to the indecision and mismanagement at home which marred the whole campaign," wrote Captain Roskill.[8]

Nevertheless, Norway was not a complete loss for the British. The campaign clearly demonstrated that a strong naval air force equipped with modern aircraft was absolutely essential for any navy operating within range of enemy land-based aircraft. The R.A.F. pilots who had flown their Hurricanes off the *Glorious* and then landed them had demonstrated that high-speed planes could indeed be operated from carriers, and the Admiralty set about obtaining such aircraft. The first experiments had also been made in radar fighter-direction during the campaign. From Norway developed, in time, the ocean-ranging fast carrier task forces of the Royal Navy, which would play a large part in winning the war.

3

Wings Over the Med

While Spitfires, Hurricanes and Messerschmitts duelled in the skies over Britain throughout the summer of 1940, the Fleet Air Arm was engaged in a bitter struggle to keep the Mediterranean open. As long as France remained in the war and Italy out of it, British convoys had passed unhampered through these waters to India and tankers brought home crude oil from the Persian Gulf. But on June 10, Mussolini took Italy into the war on the side of Germany, and the British lifeline was thus endangered. "The hand that held the dagger has struck it into the back of its neighbor," President Roosevelt said of the Italian attack on France. Because Malta was vulnerable to bombing by Italian land-based aircraft from both the North African and European coasts, the Royal Navy divided its strength between Alexandria and Gibraltar. But the island of Malta remained vital to the control of the central Mediterranean. Were Malta to fall, the Axis armies in North Africa would be more easily reinforced, and British supplies of Middle Eastern oil endangered.

The first operation conducted by the Gibraltar squadron, designated as Force H, was not against Britain's enemies, however. After the surrender of France, the British were concerned that the French Fleet anchored at Oran and nearby Mers-el-Kebir might fall into German hands. They offered the luckless French admiral Marcel Gensoul the options of continuing the fight on their side, sailing his ships to the French West Indies with reduced crews, or scuttling them. When he rejected these alternatives, Vice-Admiral Sir James Somerville, following orders from Winston Churchill, who was now Prime Minister, trained the heavy guns of his battleships on the French ships, sinking or disabling most of them.

27

Malta was a symbol of British power and prestige in the Mediterranean, and the fortress held out against German and Italian attacks throughout the war. Repeatedly, British carriers such as the *Illustrious* were sent into the Western Mediterranean to ferry planes—in this instance Hurricanes—to Malta.

The old carrier *Hermes,* after a collision damaged her at Freetown, Sierra Leone, on July 22, 1940. The first British ship designed originally as an aircraft carrier, the small *Hermes* could carry only about fifteen aircraft.

Swordfish from the *Ark Royal* met surprisingly strong resistance from American-built Curtiss-Hawks and two planes were shot down, but they managed to put four torpedoes into the French flagship *Dunkerque*, putting her out of action.

With this melancholy task out of the way, the British returned to the fight against the Axis. "You may be sure that all of us are imbued with a burning desire to get at the Italian Fleet," declared Admiral Sir Andrew B. Cunningham, commander of the ships based upon Alexandria. They soon got their chance. Early in July, Swordfish operating from Egypt torpedoed and sank an Italian destroyer and a freighter, while other Fleet Air Arm planes strafed and damaged another destroyer and transport in Tobruk harbor. A few days later, Cunningham's fleet, including the carrier *Eagle* which had embarked fifteen Swordfish and three Gladiators, was covering a convoy bound from Malta to Alexandria when an Italian convoy escorted by two battleships was sighted crossing the central Mediterranean to Libya.

Land-based Savoia-Marchetti bombers repeatedly attacked the British ships, but flew too high to do serious damage. The trio of Gladiators shot down five of them without loss. The Italian convoy was now in full retreat to the naval base at Taranto, which was located on the heel of the Italian boot. Beginning at dawn on July 9, Cunningham ordered the *Eagle*'s Swordfish to launch torpedo attacks on the Italians with the hope of slowing down their speedier ships. This was then the typical use of naval aviation; strategists did not yet believe that aircraft could sink a battleship on their own. Because of the inexperience of the aircrews, these missions were ineffective. Late in the day, the *Warspite*, having crept to within thirteen miles of the Italian flagship *Giulio Cesare*, opened up with her big guns. One of her 15-inch shells did considerable damage, and the enemy broke off the action. Both sides exchanged air attacks, with the British sinking an Italian destroyer and tanker, while the Italian high-level bombers peppered the *Eagle* and *Warspite* with near misses.

This action was the first major fleet engagement in which aircraft had taken part—albeit somewhat ineffectually on both sides. The British were handicapped by the loss of their most experienced men in the Norwegian operation, the Italians by the ineffectiveness of high-level attacks against swiftly maneuvering

An Albacore torpedo bomber makes an approach to the *Victorious* late in 1941. Earlier that year, the newly commissioned *Victorious* put to sea with a scratch complement of nine Swordfish torpedo bombers and six Fulmar aircraft, and in heavy weather launched an unsuccessful strike against the German battleship *Bismarck*.

A Sea Fox from a British cruiser off Del Ray, Florida, in December 1939. First delivered to the Royal Navy in 1927, the Sea Fox nevertheless performed extensive observation duties for British surface ships early in the war.

Slow and ugly, the all-metal Vickers Supermarine Walrus flying boat was incredibly rugged and dependable in all climates. It had an air-cooled "Pegasus" engine which proved dependable in all climates, and it could land in the water or on the deck of a carrier. Despite a top speed of only 135 mph Walruses served on observation and rescue missions throughout World War II. Indeed, some were serving in Argentina until they were retired in 1966!

Force H off Gibraltar. From left to right, the British battle cruiser *Renown* and the battleship *Malaya*, both of World War I design, escort the aircraft carrier *Ark Royal*.

ships. Perhaps the most important results of the encounter were psychological. The Italians resolved not to again risk their battleships and kept them in port at Taranto, while in the case of the British, the failure of the Italian bombers to hit their ships bred complacency about air attacks.

Despite the demands of the Battle of Britain and the threat of invasion, British air strength in the Mediterranean was gradually increased. In August, the Royal Navy received an important reinforcement: the newly commissioned 23,000-ton carrier *Illustrious*, which not only had an armored flight-deck but also carried a squadron of new Fulmar fighters. A great improvement over the Skua and Gladiator, the Fulmar carried eight machine guns like the Spitfire and Hurricane, but was still slower than most land-based fighters.

The Italians made little attempt to impede British convoys in the Mediterranean and when they did, the Fulmars shot down a goodly portion of their bombers. Diversionary attacks were

A Walrus flying boat, alongside the British heavy cruiser *Devonshire*, is hoisted on board.

launched by planes from the *Ark Royal, Eagle* and *Illustrious* whenever convoys came through the Mediterranean, and Hurricane fighters were ferried from the carriers into Malta. Until the arrival of these planes, the island's only air defense had been three Gladiators, which according to legend were known as "Faith," "Hope" and "Charity."

Anxious to get at the Italian Fleet, which was an ever-present threat to Mediterranean convoys, the British dusted off a plan of attack originally conceived by Admiral Sir David Beatty during the closing years of World War I. Frustrated by the refusal of the German High Seas Fleet to give battle in the years following Jutland, Beatty had proposed a strike by 200 torpedo planes against the German battleships as they lay in port. But the war ended before the technical obstacles to such an operation could be overcome. During the 1930s the plan had been revised for use against the Italians, and Cunningham ordered a strike against the Italian Fleet as it lay in Taranto harbor. The attack was originally to be made by Swordfish from the *Illustrious* and *Eagle* on October 21 —Trafalgar Day—but it had to be postponed because of a fire in the hangar deck of the *Illustrious.*

Early in November, American-built Maryland reconnaissance planes spotted Italy's six battleships moored in the Mar Grande, the shallow, semi-circular outer harbor of Taranto, while cruisers and destroyers were anchored in the smaller Mar Piccolo. Taranto was strongly defended by some 300 antiaircraft guns plus those on the ships, torpedo nets, galaxies of searchlights and barrage balloons—a special hazard for low-flying torpedo planes. Cunningham set the attack for the night of November 11, but the day before the ships were to sail, it was discovered that the *Eagle* had been weakened by repeated near misses from Italian bombs and sea water was seeping into her supplies of aviation fuel. Five of her Swordfish were transferred to the *Illustrious.*

Taking off in bright moonlight shortly before 2100, the first wave of twelve heavily laden Swordfish—half of them carrying torpedoes and the rest carrying bombs—rolled down the carrier's flight deck and droned off toward Taranto, about 170 miles away. They were led by Lieutenant Commander Kenneth Williamson with Lieutenant N. J. Scarlet as his observer. Making little more than 100 miles an hour, the planes were like an undirected school

The British ships *Illustrious* and *Ark Royal* steaming in the Western Mediterranean in September 1940. In November 1940, the *Illustrious* sent Swordfish torpedo bombers against the Italian naval base at Taranto and they sank one enemy battleship and damaged two others. Six months later, Swordfish from the *Ark Royal* assaulted the German battleship *Bismarck*, inflicting serious damage on her steering machinery which allowed pursuing British surface ships to catch and destroy the German raider.

The carrier *Illustrious* and the battleship *Valiant* steaming at about 20 knots in the calm Western Mediterranean after leaving Gibraltar on August 30, 1940. Four Fairey Fulmar fighters are snuggled on the *Illustrious*'s deck, their wings folded. The *Illustrious*, the first of a class of six ships, introduced radar to the British fleet. She and the *Valiant* were equipped with Type 79 sets which required a mast for the transmitting antenna and another for the receiving wires.

of fish, rising and falling as they were caught in the sudden blast of wingmates' slipstreams. There was no chance of surprise, for the Italians were ready and waiting; listening devices on the ground picked up the formation while it was still offshore. Scarlet sighted the red twinkling of antiaircraft fire while the planes were thirty miles from their target.

"That's Taranto," he told Williamson.

"Yes," the pilot replied, "they seem to be expecting us."[9]

Flares were dropped as a signal for the Swordfish to begin their dive into the volcano of gunfire that exploded about them. Down they went . . . 7,000 feet . . . 5,000 feet . . . buffeted by flak and nearly blinded by searchlights. At less than 2,000 feet above the dark waters of the Mar Grande, they slipped through the balloon barrage, Williamson's wingtips narrowly missing one of the cables. Dropping down to thirty feet, he released his torpedo at the first warship that appeared before him. It missed a destroyer and ran on to explode against the side of a much more important target, the 26,140-ton battleship *Conte di Cavour*. Water poured into a huge hole just aft of her forward gun turrets and she slowly sank into the Mar Grande until her deck was awash. However, before Williamson could make his getaway, his plane was shot down. He and Scarlet survived the crash and were taken prisoner.

Two other Swordfish made their way through the hail of anti-aircraft fire to send their tin fish into Italy's newest and largest battleship, the 35,000-ton *Littorio*, and made good their escape. Another pair nearly hit the *Andrea Doria*, their torpedoes exploding against a nearby quay with such force that the pressure caused the ship's plates to buckle. The bombers attacked vessels and installations in the Mar Piccolo and although many of their bombs failed to explode, they destroyed fuel-storage tanks, set a seaplane depot afire, and provided a diversion for the torpedo attack.

The eight Swordfish of the second wave—five carrying torpedoes and three serving as bombers—flew into a hellish crossfire from the battleships, cruisers and shore batteries. Miraculously, only one plane was shot down. Lieutenant A. F. Sutton, an observer whose plane attacked the stricken *Littorio*, reported: "She saw us and opened fire. The flash of her close-range weapons stabbed at us, first one then another, along her whole length. . . . They fired everything they had."[10] At seven hundred yards, the torpedo re-

The 35,000-ton battleship *Littorio* illustrated many of the flaws of all Italian armed forces. A sleek and graceful vessel which Mussolini often boasted would help to secure his objective of command of the sea in the Mediterranean, she was faster than all prewar and wartime British battleships. However, her military utility was slight. She was undermanned, her radio communications were abysmal, and her crew was poorly trained and led. The Italian Navy sacrificed armor protection for speed in this and other ships—some claimed they did this so that they could escape from an engagement—and even cheated in their own speed trials to increase the well-publicized ratings. Caught at her mooring in Taranto harbor in 1941 by British Swordfish bombers launched from the aircraft carrier *Illustrious*, the *Littorio* was severely damaged. This attack presaged the strike executed shortly thereafter by the Japanese against American battleships in Pearl Harbor.

lease grip was pressed. Nothing happened! By now the immense bulk of the battleship seemed to fill Sutton's vision. Feverishly, he banged on the release grip. At the last moment, the torpedo dropped away, speeding on a true course for the tall sides of the *Littorio*. Moments later, another tin fish hit the *Caio Duilio*. With all torpedoes gone, the Swordfish, dodging wildly from side to side, made their getaway through bursting shells and acrid smoke.

The next morning, when the *Illustrious* rejoined the fleet, all the ships were flying the classically understated tribute: "Maneuver well executed." Three battleships—half of Italy's battle line—had been sunk at their moorings. The *Littorio* and *Duilio* were out of action for nearly six months and the *Cavour* was beyond repair. In a few minutes, twenty obsolete aircraft had done more damage to the Italians than the entire British Grand Fleet had inflicted upon the Germans at Jutland. The attack on Taranto, made with a remarkable economy of force, conclusively demonstrated that carrier-borne aircraft would become the dominant weapon of war at sea. Half a world away, this lesson was not lost on Admiral Yamamoto and the Imperial Japanese Navy.

The Royal Navy's unchallenged domination of the Mediterranean was brief. With the Italian Navy licking its wounds and the Italian Army in full retreat in North Africa, the Germans took over the direction of the war in that theatre. Fliegerkorps X, a powerful 300-plane unit specially trained to dive-bomb ships, was transferred to the Mediterranean with direct orders from Adolf Hitler to "attack the British Navy." On January 10, 1941, it struck for the first time. The Admiralty had dispatched a large convoy loaded with supplies for the British Army in the Middle East. As

The graceful Italian battleship *Conte di Cavour* opens fire with her main battery during the Battle of Punta Stilo on July 9, 1940. Four months later, the *Cavour* was sent to the bottom of Taranto harbor by a torpedo from a British Swordfish launched off the *Illustrious*.

usual, Force H escorted it as far as Sicily, where the Mediterranean Fleet took over for the rest of the passage to Alexandria.

The day began with a torpedo attack on the convoy by the Italians. They were driven off by antiaircraft fire and Fulmar fighters from the *Illustrious*. While the British were distracted by this incident, the carrier's radar picked up a swarm of some three-dozen planes boring in from the north at 12,000 feet. They were quickly identified by those who had fought in the bitter Norwegian battles as Junkers 87s and 88s. Peeling off in flights of three, the dive bombers screamed down on the *Illustrious*, their primary target. Twisting and turning and throwing up a wall of fire, the carrier tried to evade the attackers. Eight were shot down, but she shuddered under the impact of hit after hit. In all, she was struck by six 1,100-pound bombs which set her ablaze. Only her armored flight deck saved her from sinking. Limping into Malta where temporary repairs were made, the *Illustrious* was sent to the United States for a complete refit.

The British carrier *Ark Royal* being subjected to a high-level Italian bombing attack. Contrary to legend, these attacks could often be uncomfortably accurate. Surviving many such attacks, the *Ark Royal* finally succumbed to a torpedo from a German submarine.

H.M.S. "ARK ROYAL"
1941

The bow of the British ship *Liverpool* sank after she was struck by a torpedo from Italian aircraft. Despite this damage the light cruiser was able to safely return to Alexandria.

With the departure of the *Illustrious*, the British had to limit their operations for lack of naval air cover, until the newly commissioned *Formidable* joined the Mediterranean Fleet. On March 28, Admiral Cunningham's force was again at sea, escorting a convoy of British troops bound from Egypt to Greece, when a large formation of Italian cruisers and destroyers was reported to the south of Crete. This was followed by the sighting of another enemy force, including the battleship *Vittorio Veneto*. Promised a strong air offensive by the German and Italian air forces against British air fields on Crete and Malta, the Italian Navy had left its bases with the intention of attacking the British convoys.

The *Formidable* launched six Albacore torpedo bombers—larger and faster than the Swordfish, but still biplanes—which attacked the *Veneto*, whose 15-inch guns were pounding the cruisers scouting well out in front of the British force. No hits were scored, but the Italians, whose promised air cover had not arrived, and who now realized they faced an enemy carrier, turned northwest. This ended the pressure on the British cruisers, but also meant that the Italians were drawing away from Cunningham's slower battleships.

Three Albacores and two Swordfish struck again at the *Veneto* with the hope of damaging her enough to bring her within range of the British big guns. Fortunately for the British flyers, the Italian ships had just been bombed by Greece-based R.A.F. Blenheims which, although making no hits, focused the attention of the ship's gunners on a high-level attack. Led by Lieutenant Commander Dalyell-Stead, the Albacores zoomed in on the *Veneto*. Just before his plane was hit and smashed into the sea, Dalyell-Stead released his torpedo; it found the mark, blowing a gaping hole in the battleship's stern and jamming her steering gear. Soon she was down by the stern and wallowing helplessly. Prodded by the realization that the British battleships were only three hours away, the Italian engineers worked feverishly to make repairs, and gradually won control of their vessel. Surrounded by a tight screen of cruisers and destroyers the *Veneto* limped into the approaching darkness.

As dusk fell, the British made another attack in the face of heavy defensive fire. The cruiser *Pola* was torpedoed and severely damaged; she began to lag behind the main body of ships. Two other cruisers and four destroyers were detached as an escort while the remainder of the fleet proceeded homeward with the *Veneto*. Shortly after 2200, the radar of the British battleships *Warspite, Barham* and *Valiant* picked up the hapless stragglers off the Greek coast. Within minutes, all three cruisers and two of the destroyers had been turned into flaming wrecks. The British then broke off their pursuit, afraid of getting too close to the German air bases on Sicily.

And so ended the Battle of Cape Matapan—the first battle fought on the open sea in which naval aviation had played a decisive role. Without the successes scored by the *Formidable*'s torpedo planes, none of the Italian ships would have fallen under the guns of the British battleships. In exchange for the loss of a single Albacore and its crew, the Royal Navy had sunk three cruisers, two destroyers, and badly damaged a battleship. It was, as a British admiral had said in an earlier day, "a victory . . . very necessary to England at this time." It further discouraged Italian attempts to interfere with British convoys—and the subsequent evacuations from Greece and Crete. Matapan had another curious result: realizing he needed to build up his naval air capability, Mussolini ordered the conversion of two Italian liners to aircraft carriers. Work proceeded slowly, though, and the vessels, the *Aquila* and *Sparviero*, were still in the dockyards when Italy surrendered.

Once again, however, the Royal Navy's jubilation was cut short. Quickly overrunning Greece and Yugoslavia, the Germans drove the British from Crete with heavy losses. On May 26, the *Formidable* was returning from a raid designed to relieve pressure on Crete when she was attacked by a dozen dive bombers. Before the carrier's fighters could deflect them, she was ripped so badly by three heavy bombs that she had to follow the *Illustrious* to an American shipyard for repairs. She was added to the growing list of casualties suffered by the British in trying to extricate their forces from the debacle at Crete. In a grim two-week period in May and June, sixteen ships were damaged or sunk as they tried to operate off the island in the face of Axis control of the air.

Now that the *Formidable* was gone, the full brunt of continuing British air operations in the Mediterranean was borne by the *Ark Royal* which continued to operate from Gibraltar. She covered convoys and supplied fighters for the defense of battered Malta. Repeatedly claimed sunk by the enemy, the *Ark Royal* survived to take part in a wide variety of operations that demonstrated the modern aircraft carrier's flexibility. For example, late in May, she carried two squadrons of desperately needed Hurricanes to within flying distance of Malta; three days later, she was being buffeted by Atlantic storms as she searched for the German battleship *Bismarck*.

4

Death in the Atlantic

Throughout the early years of the war, the Admiralty was haunted by the gnawing fear that German surface raiders might break out into the open sea and wreak havoc upon Britain's maritime lifeline. Enemy battleships and cruisers were carefully pinpointed and a watch established to prevent such sorties. Thus, news of the disappearance of the powerful German battleship *Bismarck* and her consort, the heavy cruiser *Prinz Eugen,* from a Norwegian fjord on May 22, 1941 was greeted with considerable anxiety. No convoy would be safe until the enemy vessels were located and brought to bay by more powerful units of the Royal Navy.

The 42,500-ton *Bismarck,* mounting eight 15-inch guns, heavily armored and with a speed of 28 knots, was the most formidable vessel afloat. She could outrun any British capital ship that she could not outfight, and posed a serious threat to the Atlantic convoys, already suffering heavy losses to the U-boats. Unless she were immediately sunk, the movement of merchant shipping across the Atlantic would have to be halted. As soon as the German ships had vanished into the Arctic mists, Admiral Sir John Tovey, commander of the Home Fleet, increased the number of vessels watching the northern passage into the Atlantic. His fastest ships, the battleship *Prince of Wales* and battle cruiser *Hood,* were sent to join the radar-fitted cruisers *Norfolk* and *Suffolk,* which were stationed in the Denmark Strait between Greenland and Iceland. Following along was a squadron which included Tovey's flagship, the battleship *King George V,* and the carrier *Victorious.* This force was not as strong as it seemed, however, for both the *Prince of Wales* and *Victorious* were newly commissioned and had not yet been shaken down. Furthermore the *Hood,* built during World War I, was lightly protected and had not been modernized.

On May 23, the *Norfolk* and *Suffolk* sighted the German ships in the Denmark Strait and flashed the information to the *Hood* and *Prince of Wales,* which came up at flank speed. The battle opened early the next morning, at a range of about 25,000 yards. Orange and black smoke engulfed the ships. The British fire was ineffective, with one of the *Prince of Wales's* turrets jamming, while the German gunnery was extremely accurate. The *Bismarck's* third salvo of 15-inch shells scored a direct hit on the *Hood,* the shells plunging through her lightly armored deck and penetrating into a magazine. She erupted with a tremendous explosion and a huge column of flame shot upward into the sky. When the dark yellow smoke had cleared, all that remained of the once-mighty battle cruiser was a few bits of debris and a spreading oil slick. Only three of her crew of 1,419 officers and men survived.

The *Bismarck* now concentrated her fire upon the *Prince of Wales,* which was hit several times. Less than a quarter-hour after the first gun of the battle had been fired, the *Prince of Wales* turned away from her formidable adversary into a protective smokescreen. But the joy of Admiral Günther Lutjens, the German commander, at having won so memorable a victory was short-lived, for two of the *Prince of Wales's* 14-inch shells had struck his vessel. Although her fighting ability was unimpaired, one of the hits had ruptured two fuel tanks. Because of the telltale loss of fuel, Lutjens cancelled the foray into the Atlantic. Detaching the *Prinz Eugen,* he ordered a course set for Brest on the French coast, the only port with a drydock that could hold his ship. As the *Norfolk* and *Suffolk* continued to shadow the *Bismarck,* Admiral Tovey pounded along behind them in the *King George V.* Other ships were detached to join the hunt and Force H, including the *Ark Royal,* was ordered up from Gibraltar.

Hoping to slow down the German vessel and bring her within range of his big guns, Tovey sent the *Victorious* ahead with an escort of cruisers. In these latitudes daylight lasted until midnight and at 2210 hours on May 24, an air strike was launched against the *Bismarck,* about 120 miles away. However, because the *Victorious* had put to sea hurriedly, only nine Swordfish had been embarked. Taking off from a pitching deck in the teeth of a near-gale, the planes, led by Lieutenant Commander Eugene Esmonde, a

The mighty German battleship *Bismarck,* in her next-to-last photograph, May 21, 1941. Displacing 42,500 tons and mounting eight 15-inch guns, she was perhaps the most awesome example of the once-proud capital ships, whose eminence was being superseded by the advent of naval airpower.

survivor of the sinking of the *Courageous,* pushed on through rain squalls toward their quarry. Most of the aircrews had little operational experience, and visibility was poor; still, they were able to find the *Bismarck.* Esmonde tried to take cover in the lowering clouds, but surprise was impossible. "It was incredible to see such obsolete-looking planes having the nerve to attack a fire-spitting mountain like *Bismarck,*" said a German officer.[11] Despite the unbroken stream of flak, the Swordfish flew to within a half-mile of the target before dropping their torpedoes. The huge vessel managed to evade all the "tin fish" except one—which exploded against her heavily armored starboard side, doing little damage.

Nevertheless, the British were closing in. The hunt appeared to be going well until early the next morning, when the pursuers lost track of the *Bismarck.* Gloom settled in on the British ships, for it was feared that she would soon be in the safe embrace of a protective screen of U-boats and land-based aircraft. For a night and a day, the suspense mounted. Where was the *Bismarck?* Force H was thrown across the course the battleship would be expected to follow to Brest—but no one knew where she actually was. When it seemed as if the pursuit would have to be called off because some of the larger ships were running short of fuel, help arrived from an unexpected source.

At 1015 hours on May 26, an R.A.F. Coastal Command Catalina (the American PBY) piloted by Ensign Leonard B. Smith of

45

the U.S. Navy, reported sighting the *Bismarck*. Although sympathetic to the British cause, the United States was officially neutral and the presence of Smith and eight other Americans as "Special Observers" with the British was top secret. For more than three hours, the plane had flown over the sea at 500 feet. It had reached the end of its search area when Smith saw a dull, black object that he gradually came to realize was a large warship. "What's that?" he asked. Before Flying Officer Dennis Briggs had a chance to reply, the *Bismarck* disclosed her identity. Shells burst all about them and the Catalina vibrated as if it were going to break apart in mid-air before Smith took evasive action. "Never been so scared in my life," he later said.[12]

The *Bismarck* had been found 690 miles from Brest—only thirty hours' steaming from safety. Although the British heaved a sigh of relief now that the enemy ship was in their net, she would escape unless slowed down. The *Ark Royal* was little more than fifty miles away and Admiral Somerville quickly ordered a strike by her torpedo planes. Fourteen Swordfish were launched at 1450, despite a gale that sent mountains of sea water pouring over the *Ark Royal*'s flight deck, which rose and plunged as much as sixty feet. About forty minutes after take-off, the aircrews spotted a ship ahead of and below them. She was a few miles to the west of the *Bismarck*'s expected position, but the vessel was obviously their target—for they had been told there was no other ship in the area. Dropping down to 400 feet, the Swordfish made out the ill-defined bulk of a warship. More than half the planes had dropped their torpedoes when it was suddenly discovered they were attacking the British cruiser *Sheffield!* She had been detailed to shadow the *Bismarck*. But what could have been a major tragedy was luckily averted. The torpedoes, armed with magnetic detonators, either exploded when they hit the towering waves or were successfully evaded by the exasperated crew of the *Sheffield*.

Time and torpedoes wasted, the crestfallen band of airmen returned to the *Ark Royal*. Within an hour, the planes had been re-armed, this time with torpedoes fitted with contact detonators, and were again airborne in search of the *Bismarck*. Darkness was falling and it was now or never. In the fading light and intermittent rain squalls, the Swordfish had some difficulty in finding the target, so they split up into sub-flights of two and three. From below, the *Sheffield* signaled, "The enemy is twelve miles dead ahead." Having found the target, the Swordfish attacked from several quarters, but with little coordination because of the heavy flak and poor visibility. Some of them found the target only because they saw the orange-red flashes of the *Bismarck*'s guns. The German ship's "decks seemed to explode into crackling flame and the sea was lashed with shot and fragments," reported one of the pilots.

Two hits were scored on the *Bismarck*. One torpedo struck her amidships, doing little damage, but the other exploded near the stern, damaging her propellers and jamming her rudder. The huge ship began circling aimlessly before her crew could bring her under control, and even then she steered erratically. Her fate had been sealed. The next morning, May 27, Tovey's battleships caught up with her, and in little more than an hour she was a shambles, her guns battered into silence. But she would not surrender and she would not sink. The cruiser *Dorsetshire* finally administered the *coup de grace* with a spread of torpedoes, and the *Bismarck* went down with her colors flying. Only 110 of her crew of more than 2,000 men survived. By slowing the *Bismarck*, the rickety Swordfish of the Fleet Air Arm had proved to be Britain's

A Blohm and Voss BV-138 seaplane picks up a moving buoy at Kirkenes, Norway. It was an unusual craft, for it had three-bladed props on the outboard engines and a four-bladed prop inboard.

margin of victory. In a symbolic gesture, two of them circled the spot where their adversary had gone down before returning to the *Ark Royal*.

* * *

The sinking of the *Bismarck* marked the last attempt by the Germans to send their biggest warships to sea as commerce raiders. Holed up in Brest, the *Gneisnau*, *Scharnhorst* and *Prinz Eugen* were frequent targets of R.A.F. bombers, but the attention of the Royal Navy was fixed on the Atlantic and the Arctic battlegrounds where Britain sought to aid its new ally, the Soviet Union. The Russian convoys were to be an important part of the Royal Navy's operations for the rest of the war—with a heavy cost in men, planes and ships. Operations in the waters above Norway and Finland were particularly hazardous because of the continual summer daylight and the proximity of German land-based aircraft.

In late July 1941, the *Victorious* and *Furious* were sent to raid the German-held ports of Petsamo and Kirkenes in northern Norway, thus disrupting vital enemy convoys from southern Norway. The element of surprise was lost, however, when a Junkers 88 sighted the squadron just as it was reaching its launching point. Twenty Albacores and nine Fulmars attacked Kirkenes while nine Albacores, nine Swordfish and six Fulmars headed for Petsamo. Both forces ran into heavy flak and determined opposition from enemy fighters. The British lost twelve aircraft and succeeded in only lightly damaging German shipping and installations. A month later, the *Victorious* and *Argus* successfully delivered thirty-nine Hurricanes destined for operations at Murmansk. On the return, German shipping was attacked, again with meager results.

The main threat to Britain was the submarine. The conquest of Norway, France and the Low Countries had given the Germans submarine bases on the entire Atlantic coast. As a consequence, the losses of British shipping began to spiral. More than 15 million tons and over 100,000 men would be lost in the Battle of the Atlantic. "The only thing that ever really frightened me during the war was the U-boat peril," Winston Churchill later acknowledged.

With their ranges extended by the ability to operate from the French coast rather than the North Sea, the submarines had a virtual free hand. The Germans also adopted highly effective new

In the summer of 1942, the *Indomitable,* escorting a convoy to the British fortress of Malta in the Mediterranean, was attacked by German Stukas which hit her with 500-pound bombs on August 12. Although she was put out of action, her 3-inch armored flight deck prevented her loss.

The British carrier *Indomitable* burning following a German dive-bombing attack on August 12, 1942.

Torpedoed by a German U-boat on November 13, 1941, the British aircraft carrier *Ark Royal* listed perilously as the destroyer *Legion* picked up nonessential members of the carrier's crew. The *Ark Royal* later foundered while under tow.

tactics. The U-boats operated in wolf-packs rather than with single boats striking at convoys, and they made their attacks on the surface at night. They also had the assistance of long-range Focke-Wulf Condor bombers which spotted convoys and sometimes attacked them on their own. For example, in October 1940, they bombed the liner *Empress of Britain* and set her afire about seventy miles off the coast of Ireland.

Constant air patrol over the convoys was the best weapon against U-boats and Condors, but Coastal Command's lumbering Sunderland flying boats were unable to reach the area of greatest danger. Besides, they were so slow that the submarines usually had ample time to dive when flying boats appeared on the scene. Even when the U.S. Navy's Atlantic Fleet joined the hunt for U-boats during the period before America entered the war, there was a 600-mile gap in the Atlantic southeast of Greenland—called the "Black Pit"—which could not be covered from either side of the ocean. Longer-range aircraft and carriers operating with the convoys were needed to fill this gap. But only nine B-24 Liberator bombers were available for this task until December 1941, and no carriers could be spared. In fact, the proud old *Ark Royal* was torpedoed and sunk by a U-boat to the east of Gibraltar on November 14, 1941, leaving the British without a carrier in the Mediterranean.

To combat the intrusion of the Condors over convoys, the Admiralty converted the old seaplane carrier *Pegasus* to carry three Fulmar fighters. This was merely a "one-shot" measure, for the planes were catapulted off the ship and if too far from a shore base, the pilots had to "ditch" in the sea and hope for rescue. As Captain Roskill has written, "their sorties demanded a cold-blooded gallantry." In all, some fifty merchantmen were converted into Catapult Armed Merchant Ships and fitted with solitary Hurricanes. They scored their first victory on August 3, 1941, when one of them shot down a Condor. "I fired five-second bursts . . . until I was forty yards astern of the enemy," said Lieutenant R. W. Everett. "Another short burst at this range and my guns were empty. I notices pieces flying off the starboard side of the Focke-Wulf and it appeared to be alight inside the fuselage." The Condor dived into the sea and Everett began to think about getting down himself. "I made two rather half-hearted attempts to bail out, but the machine nosed down and caught me when half out. I changed my mind and decided to land in the sea near H.M.S. *Wanderer* and did so. The ship sent a boat and I was extremely well looked after."[13]

A British decoy aircraft carrier that Germans mined and sunk off the east coast of England in 1940. Illustrative of the imaginative and costly British deception schemes, these decoys were built on the hulls of old merchant ships in order to deceive German photographic reconnaissance aircraft.

The rehabilitated *Indomitable* in March 1943, with Albacore torpedo planes and Seafire fighters ranged on her 3-inch-thick armored deck. One of six fleet carriers of the *Illustrious* class, the 23,000-ton *Indomitable* was smaller and carried fewer aircraft than her American contemporaries, but demonstrated the capability to survive most severe damage.

It was obvious that the CAM ship was only a stopgap measure, and the next step was the small escort carrier built on the hull of a merchantman. The first of them, the *Audacity,* was right out of the bargain basement—improvised from the captured German steamer *Hannover.* She entered service in June 1941 and achieved almost immediate success. Two of her six Grumman Martlets (the American F4F Wildcat) shot down a Condor which attacked a Gibraltar convoy and drove some others off. The operation provided clear evidence of the value of escort carriers, but it would be some time before enough of them would be available to turn the tide against the U-boat. In the meantime, the war had spread to the Pacific.

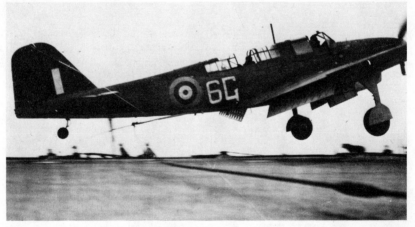

A Fairey Fulmar hooked in a carrier's arrestor wires. The Fulmar was the Fleet Air Arm's first eight-gun fighter.

5

Red Sun Rising

The Pearl Harbor raid freed the Japanese of the threat of the U.S. Pacific Fleet battleships. At the same time the Japanese fanned out from the home islands like the rays of the rising sun. They launched simultaneous blows, spearheaded by naval air units, against American and British bases in the Philippines and Malaya, and at Wake Island, Guam and Hong Kong. Complete surprise was not always possible, but the Japanese won notable victories, except at Wake Island where a tiny garrison of Marines, supported by a few Wildcat fighters, beat off the first wave of invaders. The Japanese returned in greater strength, however, and on December 23, 1941, the outnumbered defenders were overwhelmed.

The B-17 bombers that were the keystone of the American defense of the Philippines were caught on the ground by land-based Japanese Navy fighters and bombers from Formosa. Despite adequate warning of the impending strike, the bombers and defending fighters were lined up in neat rows and most of them were destroyed. The entire U.S. Army Air Force, Far East had been eliminated as an effective combat unit at a single blow.

On December 10, after a break in operations caused by bad weather, about eighty Japanese bombers escorted by fifty-two Zeros attacked the naval base at Cavite, near Manila. For two hours the bombers criss-crossed the sky 20,000 feet over the base, well out of range of its outmoded antiaircraft guns. "The entire [Navy] Yard and about one-third of the city of Cavite were ablaze from end to end," reported Admiral Thomas C. Hart, Commander in Chief of the Asiatic Fleet. Fortunately, most of Hart's ships—a handful of cruisers, destroyers and submarines—had already been dispatched for safety to the Dutch East Indies. The destruction of

Despite the reports of the remarkable performance of the Mitsubishi Zero forwarded before Pearl Harbor to Washington by Claire Chennault, head of the Flying Tigers, Allied pilots were shocked in early 1942 by the fighter's ability. The carrier-borne warplane could out-range, out-maneuver, and fly faster than any other aircraft in the Pacific, and the Zero quickly developed a reputation for invincibility. This mystique persisted until American fighter pilots learned to take advantage of the Zero's major weakness—lack of protection for the pilot and fuel.

the Cavite base, and the resulting enemy air superiority over the Philippines, made it impossible for the ships to return to contest the Japanese invasion of the island.

That same day, the Royal Navy suffered its greatest defeat of the war as Japanese torpedo planes sank the battleship *Prince of Wales* and the old battle cruiser *Repulse* off the east coast of Malaya. "In all the war I never received a more direct shock," Winston Churchill later confessed. "As I turned and twisted in bed the full horror of the news sank in upon me. There were no British or American capital ships in the Indian Ocean or the Pacific . . . Over this vast expanse of waters Japan was supreme, and we everywhere were weak and naked."[14]

Before the war, British strategy in the Far East called for a strong battle fleet in East Asian waters to deter Japanese aggression. As late as August 1941 the Admiralty discussed plans to send six capital ships and an aircraft carrier to Singapore. But the requirements of the European conflict made such a transfer impossible, and only after considerable pressure from Churchill did the

Admiralty agree to send the *Prince of Wales* and the *Repulse* as tokens.

Neither ship was well-fitted for the task assigned it. Like all the battle cruisers left over from World War I, the *Repulse* was thin-skinned and her antiaircraft armament was outmoded. The *Prince of Wales* was badly ventilated and unsuitable for extended service in the tropics. The new carrier *Indomitable* had also been earmarked for Force Z, as the unit was to be designated, but she ran aground in the West Indies while engaged in training exercises. Rear Admiral Sir Tom Phillips, the former Vice-Chief of the Naval Staff who commanded the squadron, was an experienced staff officer but had not yet held a command at sea under wartime conditions.

On the evening of December 8, Phillips left Singapore with his two big ships and four destroyers to attack a Japanese invasion fleet reported to be putting troops ashore at Singora in the Gulf of Siam. The Admiral asked the R.A.F. to provide reconnaissance in advance of his force and fighter protection while it was in action. But the hard-pressed airmen, who had already lost many of their aircraft and airfields to the Japanese, replied they could not supply such support.

The ships were not to be left completely without air cover, however. Phillips was informed that a squadron of Brewster Buffalo fighters would be kept in readiness at Sembawang, near Singapore, to answer any call for help. He was also warned that the Japanese were assembling a sizable force of torpedo bombers near Saigon. Perhaps basing his judgment on the limited range of the Fleet Air Arm's Swordfish, Phillips assumed that no torpedo plane could cover the 400 miles from Indochina to the invasion beaches. In any event, convinced that he could not remain in port while enemy landings were taking place, he went to sea. He would rely upon surprise, and upon the speed and antiaircraft batteries of his ships, for protection.

Maintaining radio silence and evading Japanese minefields and submarine patrols, Force Z steamed northward through the damp and clammy tropical night and into the next day, December 9, without incident. At first, fortune seemed to favor the British. A Japanese reconnaissance plane which flew over Singapore that morning mistakenly reported that the *Prince of Wales* and *Re-*

pulse had not left the harbor. And during the mid-afternoon, a submarine sighted the ships at sea but its signal was delayed in reaching Japanese headquarters. Believing the false report that the British were still in port, the planes of the Japanese Navy's 22nd Air Flotilla at its airfields near Saigon prepared to attack the ships. "Everyone was busy investigating the water depths of the Singapore Naval Base, the best directions from which to attack, and the most advantageous flight formations to utilize," Lieutenant Sadoa Takai later recalled.[15]

Consisting of three wings—the Genzan, Kanoya and Mihoro Corps—the 22nd Air Flotilla was one of the most highly rated units in the Japanese Navy. Most of the pilots and air crews had seen service in China. The flotilla had a strength of 141 aircraft: 105 twin-engine Nells and Bettys, which could be employed as both high-level and torpedo bombers, as well as 36 Zero fighters. When

The Nakajima B5N2 Kate torpedo plane was the first carrier-borne monoplane. With a top speed of 235 mph and a range of 1,238 miles, the Kate was vastly superior to its contemporaries, the American Devastator and the British Swordfish.

the submarine's report of the sighting of the British vessels at sea was finally received at Saigon, the Japanese were startled and confused. Had the *Prince of Wales* and *Repulse* actually left Singapore? Or were they still lying in port? The fate of the entire Japanese invasion force lay in the balance because the British vessels' big guns would make short work of the transports and supply ships.

Intelligence officers carefully scrutinized the pictures taken that morning by the reconnaissance aircraft which were now available and the mystery was resolved. Because of the great height from which the photographs were made, two large cargo vessels had been mistaken for the warships. Orders were immediately given for the landing force—which had already put most of its men ashore at Singora—to disperse. Even though night was falling, every available ship and plane was ordered to search for the British ships.

Fifty-three bombers, most armed with torpedoes, took off from Saigon into the darkening sky and headed south. Visibility was poor and in their haste to attack, the Japanese had not established methods of identifying their own ships. The clouds seemed to stretch endlessly over the ocean, and the planes flew farther and farther southward without sighting the enemy ships. Eventually, the pilot of one of the low-flying planes saw two bright lanes of foam which he took to be the wakes of the British vessels. Climbing away, he got off a sighting report and added: "We have dropped a flare bomb."[16]

The rest of the bombers sped toward the position flashed to them, with the pilots fearing that the attack had already been launched without them. "We extracted the last ounce of power from our motors trying to make the airplanes go faster and faster," said Takai. Before they arrived, however, it was discovered that the ship about to be attacked was the *Chokai*, flagship of Vice Admiral Jisaburo Ozawa's cruiser force. Badly shaken by the narrow escape, the Japanese ordered an end to the search until daybreak to prevent further mishaps. The weary aircrews returned to their base, but because of a shortage of torpedoes, they could not dump them into the sea. And so the frustrating day was climaxed by a harrowing night landing with live torpedoes.

In the meantime, the British squadron had again been sighted.

The *Prince of Wales* (top) and *Repulse* leaving Singapore for the last time on December 8, 1941.

Just as darkness was falling, the *Prince of Wales*'s radar had picked up three aircraft which turned out to be float planes launched by Ozawa's cruisers. Remaining well out of range of British guns, they reported the squadron's position before disappearing. Realizing that all chance of surprising the Japanese invasion fleet had been lost, Admiral Phillips reluctantly ordered his ships to return to Singapore. Neither side knew it, but only five miles had separated the British from the Japanese cruisers—and what might well have been one of the decisive sea battles of World War II.

The last of the Japanese aircraft and their exhausted crews had not landed until well after midnight, but at dawn on December 10, 94 bombers were ready to take off. Nine of the Nells were earmarked for reconnaissance, 25 were armed with torpedoes and 34 carried bombs. An additional 26 Bettys were also fitted with torpedoes. But where were the *Prince of Wales* and *Repulse?* Phillips's change in course to the south had been detected during the night by a Japanese submarine that had fired a spread of five torpedoes at the speeding ships—all of which missed—but it had been unable to keep up with them. At dawn, the Japanese launched the reconnaissance aircraft toward Singapore with the hope of finding the British vessels. The bombers would follow later and be guided to the target.

Although almost all the air crews were veterans, none of them had participated in a torpedo strike. One young pilot asked Lieutenant Takai about the angle of attack to be followed and was told that if he became confused it was best to "fly very low and aim your torpedo directly at the bow of the vessel under attack." Having stowed their flight rations in their planes—rice cake coated with bean paste and flasks of thick, sweetened coffee—the pilots began taking off at 0625. Visibility was good and the Nells and Bettys climbed to 10,000 feet where in formations of eight or nine, they settled in on a southerly course.

But Force Z was no longer headed directly back to its base. During the night, Admiral Phillips had received a signal from Singapore that the Japanese were landing at Kuantan, about 180 miles north of the island. Seizing an opportunity to retrieve something from his sortie, Phillips ordered a detour to Kuantan. Radio silence was maintained, however, and no attempt was made to inform headquarters of his decision. He apparently assumed that the staff at Singapore would anticipate his reaction to the signal warning of the landing, and would automatically send fighter cover for the squadron. But the fighters earmarked for the protection of the *Repulse* and *Prince of Wales* remained on the ground. Arriving off Kuantan that morning, the British found the landing report a false alarm, but instead of immediately pressing on to Singapore, Phillips spent several hours investigating the situation. It was a fatal mistake.

The Japanese had almost reached Singapore without sighting

their quarry. "What is the matter with our reconnaissance planes?" Lieutenant Takai angrily asked himself. "Still no sign of the enemy." With their fuel dwindling, several aircraft were forced to return to Saigon and the rest would soon have to follow. Suddenly, the long-awaited signal was flashed from one of the searchers: "Sighted two enemy battleships. Seventy nautical miles southeast of Kuantan." Turning northward on the new bearing, the bombers raced to the reported position. As he strained for a sight of the *Prince of Wales* and *Repulse*, Takai "became nervous and shaky. . . . It was exactly like the sensation one feels before entering a contest in an athletic meet. At exactly 1:03 P.M. (1133 Singapore time) a black spot was sighted directly beneath the cloud ahead of us. . . . Yes—it was the enemy!"[17]

Eight Nells swept over the *Repulse*, low enough so men on deck could see the bombs fall. It was a harrowing moment but despite several near misses only one struck the battle cruiser, exploding on her starboard side and doing little damage. Ten minutes later, two squadrons of torpedo planes, including the one commanded by Lieutenant Takai, bore in on the *Prince of Wales*. Used to the lumbering Swordfish, the flagship's gunners were amazed at the speed of the Japanese approach. "The air was filled with white smoke, bursting shells, and the tracers of antiaircraft guns and machine guns," Takai declared. "As if pushed down by the fierce barrage thrown up by the enemy, I descended to just above the water's surface. The airspeed indicator registered more than 200 knots. I do not remember at all how I was flying the airplane, how I was aiming, and at what distance we were from the ship when I dropped the torpedo. . . ."[18]

In all, nine torpedoes sped toward the ship, the white line of bubbles clearly visible in the mirror-like sea. "Suddenly, there was a most terrific jolt accompanied by a loud explosion," reported a Royal Marine officer. "A vast column of water and smoke shot up into the air to a height of about 200 feet . . . at least one torpedo had hit us." The *Prince of Wales* immediately began to lose way, her speed dropping from 25 to 15 knots, and she took on a strong list. The electrical supply failed in various parts of the ship and soon there were no lights, no power for many of the guns, and no forced ventilation below deck. The torpedo had exploded on the battleship's port side near the stern, snapping one of her propeller shafts and tearing open the shaft passage. Water poured into her hull with a tremendous rush. A single torpedo had transformed an efficient and powerful fighting machine into a crippled hulk.

Two formations of torpedo planes now attacked the *Repulse*. Undeterred by the weak barrage thrown up by the battle cruiser's inadequate antiaircraft guns, the Japanese pressed in to drop their torpedoes at point-blank range. Only the magnificent shiphandling of Captain W. G. Tennant saved the *Repulse* from destruction. Frantically twisting and turning as if she were a destroyer, the old ship managed to evade every one of the torpedoes. A brief lull followed in which Tennant, having heard nothing from the *Prince of Wales*, broke radio silence and notified Singapore that Force Z was under attack. The squadron of Buffaloes kept in readiness at Sembawang was immediately ordered into the air, but they were almost an hour's flying time from the scene of the battle.

Just as the fighters were taking off, twenty-six Betty torpedo planes attacked the ships. Six of the planes approached the *Prince of Wales* from various directions. A few guns opened fire, some of them trained by crews that frantically hauled the barrels around with chains or ropes, due to the lack of power. With the vessel's steering gear out of action, there was little the British sailors could do except watch the enemy planes approach in horrified fascination. Four torpedoes struck the battleship on her starboard side in quick succession, one of them passing through both sides of the bow.

The Japanese now turned their full attention to the *Repulse*, about four miles away. Eight more Bettys attacked her starboard side and again Captain Tennant managed to avoid their torpedoes, but one launched by aircraft that unexpectedly appeared on the battle cruiser's port side struck her amidships. The *Repulse*'s luck had run out. Skillfully attacking her from various directions, another nine Japanese aircraft put four more torpedoes into the valiant old ship. In little more than an hour and a half, the *Prince of Wales* and *Repulse* had been hit by a total of ten torpedoes and were sinking.

The *Repulse* went first. Only eleven minutes after she had been struck by the first torpedo, she rolled over and sank, leaving the sea covered with struggling men, debris and great globs of oil. The *Prince of Wales* took longer to die, which allowed the destroyers,

63

Following the Japanese attack on Pearl Harbor, Admiral Chuichi Nagumo supported landings at Wake and Rabaul in the Pacific and at key points in the Netherlands East Indies. Nagumo then took his task force against Darwin, Australia and into the Indian Ocean against the British base at Tricomalee, Ceylon. In the move into the East Indies, Nagumo's forces sank the British aircraft carrier *Hermes*.

working unhindered by the Japanese, to take off survivors. She floated upside down with her flat bottom exposed before her bow reared into the air and she plunged stern-first to the bottom. Three minutes before the *Prince of Wales* sank, the Buffaloes reached the scene of the disaster. The victorious Japanese, their fuel low, had already gone and the fighters—which might have made a difference if summoned earlier by Admiral Phillips—could do nothing except circle aimlessly over the desolate scene. Of the 2,921 men aboard the two ships, 840 did not survive. Among the dead was Tom Phillips.

Following on the heels of Pearl Harbor, the destruction of Force Z had far-reaching tactical and strategic effects. Not only the U.S.

Navy, but now the Royal Navy, had had its Pacific battle fleet decimated by Japanese aircraft. Unhindered by Allied naval power, the Japanese were free to proceed with the conquest of Southeast Asia and the East Indies. With the loss of only three airplanes, the Japanese had brought an end to the dominance of the seas by the battleship and the big gun. For the first time, capital ships had been sunk by aircraft while underway on the high seas. The surface fleet without air cover had been rendered obsolete.

*　*　*

Like the tentacles of an octopus, the Japanese forces, having captured Singapore, reached south from the Malay Peninsula to grasp the rich oilfields of the Dutch East Indies. Japanese air and surface superiority was so complete that there was little that the hastily assembled American, British, Dutch and Australian fleet could do to oppose enemy landings. Without hope of reinforcement and with its bases under constant air bombardment, this force was overwhelmed in a series of forlorn battles. Among the ships lost was the old seaplane tender *Langley*, which had been the U.S. Navy's first aircraft carrier. She was caught at sea while ferrying a load of Army P-40s to Java and sunk by Japanese bombers. "Mamma said there would be days like this," tapped out a radioman before abandoning ship. "She must have known!"[19]

Although most of the Allied ships were sunk by surface forces, Japanese naval aircraft, flown from the four carriers that had taken part in the Pearl Harbor raid, made a significant contribution to victory in the East Indies. They destroyed Allied bases, damaged ships, wiped out stocks of stores, crates of aircraft fuel and ammunition, and wore out the crews. Float planes catapulted off Japanese cruisers played a vital role in locating the enemy's ships during the battles in the Java Sea. Carrier planes also brought the war to Australia. On February 18, 1942, the Japanese attacked Port Darwin on the north coast of the island continent, the main staging area for the supplying of Allied forces in Java. They sank eight ships, including an American destroyer, accounted for eighteen planes and put the base out of action—all at the cost of only two aircraft.

From their newly won bases at Singapore and Java, the Japanese were in a position to threaten Britain's lifelines in the Indian

The old British carrier *Hermes*, the first British ship designed from the keel up as an aircraft carrier, sinks in the Bay of Bengal. Caught without air cover by Japanese aircraft from Nagumo's task force, the *Hermes* was dispatched in short order off Ceylon in April 1942.

Ocean. Ceylon and the coast of India lay open to invasion, the flow of tankers coming out of the Persian Gulf was endangered, and the Japanese could eventually control the seas off the east coast of Africa, thus cutting off the main supply route to the British army in the Middle East. The British quickly assembled a new Eastern Fleet built around the ubiquitous *Warspite*, four obsolete World War I battleships, and the carriers *Indomitable*, *Formidable* and the smaller *Hermes*. Vice-Admiral Sir James Somerville, who had done yeoman service in the Mediterranean with Force H, was placed in command. Just after Somerville had taken over at the end of March 1942, word was received that a Japanese force of five carriers and four battleships under Admiral Chuichi Nagumo had entered the Indian Ocean. The Japanese hoped to catch the British at anchor at Colombo, Ceylon—just as they had caught the Americans, at Pearl Harbor.

Realizing that his ships were inferior to the enemy force and vastly outnumbered in aircraft, Somerville thought it wise to retreat to an emergency base at Addu Atoll, some 600 miles south of Ceylon. On Easter Sunday, April 5, the Japanese struck Colombo with 315 planes. They aimed at the shops, harbor installations and oil-tank farms, and caused severe damage. Most of the ships in the port had been sent to sea, however. British fighters, although late in getting off, shot down seven of the attackers. Learning of the raid, Somerville left his four older ships at Addu Atoll and raced ahead, hoping to catch up with the Japanese so he could launch a night torpedo attack.

Steaming toward Somerville were the cruisers *Cornwall* and *Dorsetshire*, which had escaped from Colombo. They were spotted and attacked by eighty Japanese dive bombers. Admiral Nagumo's staff could hear the exchange of radio messages between the commander of the dive-bomber force and his pilots:

"Sighted enemy vessels."

"Get ready to go in."

"Air Group, 1st Cardiv, take the first ship; Air Group, 2nd Cardiv, take the second ship."

There was a short period in which no messages were heard. Then:

"Ship Number One has stopped. Dead in the water. Listing heavily."

"Ship Number Two is aflame."

"Ship Number One has sunk."

"Ship Number Two has sunk."[20]

Only nineteen minutes were required to dispose of the hapless cruisers.

Unable to locate the Japanese carriers and concerned about the many traces of enemy air reconnaissances over his own ships, Somerville turned back the next morning to rejoin the rest of his fleet. It was just as well, because his Albacores and Swordfish would have been no match for the Zeros which would have been waiting for them. Meantime, Nagumo attacked Trincomalee, on the east coast of Ceylon. As at Colombo, the harbor had been emptied of shipping and the Japanese concentrated on the port installations, doing considerable damage. The carrier *Hermes*, which had been hustled to sea without fighters, was caught by enemy dive bombers while trying to return to port. They made short work of her and an escorting destroyer. Low on fuel, Nagumo did not follow up his advantage, however, and retired through the Malacca Straits to Singapore.

The Imperial Japanese Navy—with its carriers in the vanguard—now commanded the seas from Hawaii to Ceylon.

6

Coral Sea and Midway

Turning into the wind at daybreak on April 18, 1942, the carrier *Hornet* prepared to unleash a strange and ungainly brood. Sixteen twin-engined Army B-25 bombers lumbered down her spray-swept flight deck, and after groping their way into the air, headed for Tokyo, 668 miles away. Navy planes lacked the range to carry the war to the Japanese home islands, so the B-25s had been chosen for this mission. The surprise raid on Tokyo and other Japanese cities was part of the "defensive-offensive" strategy developed by Admiral Ernest J. King, the newly appointed Commander-in-Chief, U.S. Fleet, "The 'defensive-offensive' may be paraphrased as 'hold what you've got and hit them where you can'," said King.[21]

Admiral Chester W. Nimitz, who had taken over in Pearl Harbor as Commander-in-Chief, Pacific Fleet, had begun the new year with carrier strikes against advanced Japanese bases in the Gilbert and Marshall islands. On February 1, a task force under the pugnacious Rear Admiral William F. Halsey, Jr., who flew his flag in the *Enterprise*, raided Kwajalein in the Marshalls, sinking a transport and two other ships and damaging several smaller craft. Similar attacks were launched on Wake and Marcus islands, and on February 21 the *Lexington* task force raided the newly seized Japanese base at Rabaul, on the island of New Britain to the northeast of Australia. Aircraft from the Japanese 25th Air Flotilla tried to interfere and the first air battle between American and Japanese naval planes took place within full view of the crew of the "Lady Lex," who waved and yelled encouragement to the pilots. Lieutenant Edward H. O'Hare shot down five Kate torpedo bombers, becoming the Navy's first ace of the war and win-

The large American aircraft carrier *Saratoga,* launching TBF Avenger torpedo planes late in the war. Although the oldest U. S. Navy carrier afloat, the *Saratoga,* which displaced 33,000 tons, was still the largest. Converted from a battle cruiser in the early 1920s, she carried 100 aircraft and was originally armed with eight 8-inch guns; however, by the end of the conflict these were replaced by smaller, but more useful, 5-inch guns.

ning the Medal of Honor. The operation clearly showed that American pilots and carrier aircraft were quite capable of holding their own with their Japanese counterparts.

The Tokyo raid was the most spectacular of these early attacks. The Army Air Force pilots, under the command of Lieutenant Colonel James H. Doolittle, a pioneer speed and test pilot, had been given intensive training in short take-offs. They were not trained, however, in carrier landings, for they were to fly to air fields in China, about 1,100 miles away. Halsey, whose task force met the *Hornet* at sea, watched the B-25s take off from the bridge of the *Enterprise:*

The wind and the sea were so strong that morning that green water was breaking over the carrier's ramps. Jimmy led his squadron off. When his plane buzzed down the *Hornet's* deck at 0725, there wasn't a man topside who didn't help sweat him into the air. One pilot hung on the brink of a stall until we nearly çatalogued his effects. . . ."[22]

Admiral Ernest J. King

Complete surprise was achieved by the Doolittle raiders, and of the eighty airmen involved, all but nine survived. Three were executed by the Japanese after being taken prisoner. But, like the hit-and-run raids on Kwajalein, Wake, and Marcus Island, the damage was slight. Nevertheless, these strikes lifted sagging American morale, kept the enemy guessing, and provided a valuable test of fast carrier tactics.

The Japanese completed the conquest of the Greater East Asia Co-Prosperity Sphere in half the time and with far less casualties than they had anticipated. Now it was time to consolidate their conquests and strengthen their defense perimeter against the

71

Admiral Chester W. Nimitz is shown with (from left to right) Lieutenant General D. C. Emmons, Vice Admiral F. J. Fletcher, Admiral Raymond A. Spruance, and Lieutenant General Simon Bolivar Buckner at Admiral Nimitz's Pearl Harbor headquarters, *circa* 1943.

Allied assault that was certain to be launched against it one day. But Japan's top strategists were infected with "Victory Disease" and embarked on a new campaign of conquest in the Southwest Pacific. Their goal was to isolate Australia by capturing Port Moresby on New Guinea, and Tulagi in the Solomons. Port Moresby was a thorn in the side of the Japanese because it was a base from which Allied planes could strike back, while Tulagi was to be a Japanese staging area for the capture of New Caledonia and Fiji.

The Americans, however, had broken the Japanese naval code, and were aware that the enemy was sending two invasion forces with three carriers into the Coral Sea. The large carriers *Shokaku* and *Zuikaku* were covering the Port Moresby invasion force while the smaller *Shoho* was with the Tulagi group. Admiral Nimitz mobilized all his available strength—the *Yorktown* task force under Rear Admiral Frank Jack Fletcher and the *Lexington* group under Rear Admiral Aubrey W. Fitch—with Fletcher in overall command. Halsey was also ordered to join them with the *Enterprise* and *Hornet* as soon as he returned from the Tokyo raid. Between them the *Lexington* and *Yorktown* embarked 143 planes—Wildcat fighters which had proven slower and less nimble than the Zeros, the durable SBD Dauntless dive bombers, and the hopelessly outclassed TBD Devastator torpedo planes.

The curtain rose on the Battle of the Coral Sea on May 3, 1942, as the Japanese captured Tulagi and established a seaplane base there. The following day, the *Yorktown* launched three successive

The basic American fighter in the first year of Pacific war: Grumman F4Fs diving to attack the Japanese fleet during the Battle of Midway.

Admiral King's early strategy in the Pacific War was to block and raid the Japanese as they advanced across the Central and South Pacific. An assistant, Captain Francis "Frog" Low, proposed a sweeping raid against Tokyo, which would throw Japanese strategy completely off balance. On April 18, 1942, AAF B-25B bombers, under the command of Colonel Jimmy Doolittle, warmed up on the flight deck of the *Hornet*, before making their attack on Tokyo.

attacks on the beachhead, but the results were disappointing. Most of the Japanese ships had already departed, although a destroyer was badly damaged and eventually sank, and some small craft and five seaplanes were destroyed by the SBDs and TBDs. Fletcher then rejoined Fitch, and for the next two days they searched the placid sea for the Port Moresby invasion force. On May 7 the two fleets made contact. At 0815, an American reconnaissance plane reported the sighting of "two carriers and four heavy cruisers." Believing that this was the main Japanese carrier force, Admiral Fletcher ordered a strike by ninety-three aircraft from the *Lex-*

The nose of an AAF B-25B Mitchell bomber which is waiting on the deck of the *Hornet* before taking off to strike Tokyo.

ington and *Yorktown*. These planes had almost reached the target when it was discovered that the report was garbled—the scout plane had sighted only two cruisers and two destroyers. Gambling that the invasion fleet must be in the vicinity, Fletcher allowed the strike to continue.

This gamble was rewarded when the *Shoho* was discovered not

An AAF Mitchell takes off from the *Hornet* on April 18, 1942. The commander of the operation, Vice Admiral Halsey, ordered the bombers into the air before he had originally planned, on the belief that his task force had been sighted by Japanese reconnaissance. Later, President Roosevelt was asked from where the planes had been launched and he replied, "Shangri-La," the name for his mountain retreat in Maryland. When new carriers were being named in 1943, he insisted that one be christened with this name.

far from the position of the original target. "Scratch one flattop!" an exuberant SBD pilot radioed the *Lexington,* as the *Shoho,* smothered by thirteen bomb hits and ripped by seven torpedoes, quickly went to the bottom. Upon receiving news of the loss of the *Shoho,* the Japanese ordered the Port Moresby invasion force to turn back until the Americans had been cleared from the area. That same morning, aircraft from the *Shokaku* and *Zuikaku* sank what they thought was a carrier and cruiser. The ships turned out to be the fleet oiler *Neosho* and the destroyer *Sims*—and the Japanese pilots had been so busy disposing of them, they had not spotted the nearby American carriers.

Late in the day, Rear Admiral Takeo Takagi, commander of the Japanese carrier force, sent twenty-seven planes to strike the American carriers, but the Japanese missed the ships because of approaching darkness and poor visibility. Nine of the planes were shot down by American combat air patrols that had been vectored in on them by radar. Several Japanese pilots mistook the American carriers for their own in the darkness, and some even tried to land on the *Yorktown*. One fell victim to the carrier's guns and the others were driven off. Eleven crashed into the sea as they tried to make night landings on their own carriers. Thus, only six of the twenty-seven planes returned safely.

Dawn on May 8 found the two carrier forces—now evenly matched in the number of ships and planes—about 175 miles apart. The ensuing battle consisted primarily of an exchange of carrier strikes. With torpedo and dive bombers from the *Yorktown* leading the attack, the Americans struck the first blow. The *Zuikaku* had disappeared into a sudden rain squall so they concentrated on

The SBD Dauntless was the mainstay of the U. S. Navy's dive-bombing force throughout the war in the Pacific. The Dauntless had a maximum speed of 275 mph, a range of 1,000 miles, and could carry a ½-ton bomb. The Americans built nearly 6,000 of this type during the hostilities. Late in the war the Curtiss SB2C Helldiver, a type with only marginal improvements, began to replace the Dauntless.

Vice Admiral Frank Jack Fletcher

the *Shokaku*. Nine TBDs went in but American torpedoes were notoriously slow and had a tendency to misfire, so the carrier was unharmed. The SBDs had better luck. Two bombs damaged the *Zuikaku*'s flight deck so badly that she could not handle her planes.

In the meantime, the Japanese struck at the American carriers, attacking while some of the seventeen Wildcats of the combat air patrol were refueling. The *Yorktown*, which evaded eight torpedoes, was hit by a heavy bomb and the *Lexington* was shaken by a terrific explosion. Fumes from her aviation-fuel supply lines, ruptured by the bombing, had been ignited by a chance spark. With flames engulfing his vessel, Captain Frederick C. Sherman was finally forced to give the order to abandon ship. Most of the crew of some 3,000 men were saved, however, before the blazing hulk was sunk by her escorting destroyers to make certain that she did not fall into enemy hands.

Although sporadic action continued the next day, the Battle of the Coral Sea was over. The first naval action in history in which surface ships did not exchange a single shot—or, indeed, even see

With perforated combination flaps and dive brakes plainly visible, an **SBD3** Dauntless dive bomber releases a ½-ton bomb. Able to absorb considerable punishment, the Dauntless suffered the lowest loss rate of any U. S. Navy aircraft type in the Pacific war.

one another—was a tactical victory for the Japanese, but a strategic victory for the Americans. The Americans had lost three ships, including the "Lady Lex," and seventy-seven planes while the Japanese lost the less valuable *Shoho* and several smaller vessels as well as ninety-seven aircraft. But the attempt to capture Port Moresby had been turned back—the first time a Japanese thrust had been blunted—and the seaplane base at Tulagi had been neutralized. The *Yorktown* was soon back in action, but the *Zuikaku's* lost planes and experienced air crews could not be immediately replaced, and the *Shokaku* would require long months of repair. Thus, neither Japanese carrier was available for Midway, the most crucial battle of the Pacific war.

✿   ✿   ✿

Admiral Isoroku Yamamoto, Commander-in-Chief of the Combined Fleet, and the man who had planned the Pearl Harbor attack, had no illusions about Japan's easily winning the war, despite the floodtide of early Japanese victories. Realizing that Japan had to secure a decisive victory before the industrial might of

A crewman readies the rear cockpit .30-cal. machine-gun mount on a Douglas SBD3 Dauntless dive bomber aboard the carrier *Enterprise* before the raid on Wake Island on February 24, 1942. These raids were intended to harass and discomfort the Japanese offensive—a strategy that succeeded.

Squadron commanding officer's F4F3 Wildcat from the aircraft carrier *Hornet* before that ship was withdrawn by Admiral Ernest J. King from the Atlantic to the Pacific to carry out the famous Tokyo Raid. With a top speed of 330 mph, the Wildcat was slower and less maneuverable than the Zero, her main opponent. Only by devising tactics that optimized the Wildcat's advantages, heavy firepower and rugged construction, could F4F fighter pilots effectively combat the Japanese.

America could be mobilized, he had declared in 1941: "If I am told to fight regardless of the consequences, I shall run wild for the first six months or a year, but I have utterly no confidence for the second and third years of the fighting."[23] He was obsessed with the need to complete the work of Pearl Harbor by smashing the U.S. Pacific Fleet before Japan's strength began to ebb. He chose Midway Island, about 1,100 miles to the west of Pearl Harbor, as the place for this climactic battle, and devised an elaborate plan to draw the Americans into a trap.

Like most Japanese naval planning, the Midway operation was a complex blend of stealth, ruse and division of forces intended to keep the enemy off balance. Yamamoto divided his fleet into three major parts: a striking force of four carriers, the *Akagi, Hiryu, Kaga* and *Soryu,* commanded once again by Admiral Nagumo, who had led these same ships in the Pearl Harbor raid; a dozen

The first American carrier named *Lexington* was an extraordinary ship. Her captains had pioneered carrier tactics in the 1930s and it was to her and her sister ship, the *Saratoga*, that Admiral King turned after Pearl Harbor to hold the line in the South Pacific. Attempting to bar the Japanese from the Coral Sea, the *Lexington* was hit on May 8, 1942 by several enemy bombs and from three to five torpedoes, but damage control measures seemed effective and the carrier began to steam back to Pearl Harbor. But six hours later, a spark ignited gas fumes, her insides blew up, and she was abandoned and finally sunk by five torpedoes from the nearby American destroyer *Phelps*.

transports, carrying 5,000 troops for the occupation of Midway, and escorted by two battleships and the light carrier *Zuiho*; and the main body, consisting of seven battleships, including Yamamoto's flagship, the powerful 60,000-ton *Yamato*, which was armed with 18-inch guns. This armada was preceded to sea by a diversionary force consisting of the carriers *Ryujo* and *Junyo*, a pair of cruisers, and some transports assigned to bombard Dutch Harbor in the Aleutians and to seize Adak, Attu and Kiska. The Aleutians raid was designed to lure the Pacific Fleet to the north while Midway was being occupied. When the Americans learned of the ruse and hastened south, they would be destroyed by Yamamoto's carriers and battleships.

Intercepted Japanese code messages made it clear that the Japanese were planning a massive operation in the central Pacific, but Admiral Nimitz was uncertain where the blow would fall. The

82

The *Lexington* burns after Japanese hits in the Battle of the Coral Sea.

enemy's radio traffic made numerous reference to "AF," which some officers were certain was Midway. Lieutenant Commander Joseph J. Rochefort, in charge of the decoding operation at Pearl Harbor, devised a plan to smoke out Japanese intentions. Nimitz approved, and Midway was instructed to transmit a message to Pearl Harbor in plain English stating that its water-distilling plant was out of commission. Two days later, a Japanese message reported that "AF" was short of water.

Forewarned of the planned Japanese attack on Midway, Nimitz redoubled efforts to strengthen the defenses of the island and brought every available ship and plane to the central Pacific. Working around the clock, the dockyard at Pearl Harbor in three days repaired damage to the *Yorktown* that would have required three months in peacetime. Admiral Halsey was ordered to bring the *Enterprise* and *Hornet* back from the Coral Sea. By June 1, Nimitz had a fleet of three carriers, eight cruisers, fourteen destroyers and about twenty submarines—about half the size of the Japanese fleet—deployed to the northeast of Midway. The fleet was divided into two task forces, one commanded by Admiral Fletcher, who once again had overall command, and the other by Rear Admiral Raymond A. Spruance, one of the Navy's leading

Another photograph of "Lady Lex" going down after the Battle of the Coral Sea. The American check to the Japanese strike into the Coral Sea, along with the Tokyo Raid, forced the Japanese to reorient their priorities and move into the Central Pacific in an attempt to force a "decisive engagement" with the American carrier task forces.

strategists. Spruance had replaced Halsey, who had been hospitalized with a skin rash. Refusing to be decoyed by the planned Aleutian raid, Nimitz had assigned a small cruiser force to deal with it. "Inflict maximum damage on the enemy," Nimitz told his commanders.

The Battle of Midway began in the fog-shrouded Aleutians, where on June 3, Japanese aircraft bombed Dutch Harbor, severely damaging the installations there. The cruisers dispatched by Nimitz to the Aleutians were outmaneuvered and four days later the Japanese landed troops on bleak Attu and Kiska. Ignoring these moves, however, Nimitz singlemindedly concentrated his attention on the events unfolding in the central Pacific. While the attack on Dutch Harbor was underway, a PBY piloted by Ensign Jewell H. Reid scoured the central Pacific about 700 miles to the west of Midway searching for the advancing enemy. " Do you see what I see?" he asked his copilot as he spotted a sizeable formation of ships. "You're damned right I do!" was the reply.[24] Reid

In May 1942, a tremendous explosion tossed aircraft skyward and wrenched the *Lexington*. Shortly thereafter, the 33,000 ton carrier sank in the Coral Sea.

had sighted the Japanese transports, but heavy cloud cover prevented him from determining the exact composition of the approaching force. But when his report reached Pearl Harbor, Admiral Nimitz greeted it with "a bright white smile," according to an aide. A flight of Army B-17s stationed on Midway attacked the transports in the belief that they were part of the enemy's main force. The inexperienced pilots claimed damage to two battleships or heavy cruisers, but in actuality, they did not score any hits.

Early the next morning, June 4, another PBY spotted the Japanese carrier strike force about 200 miles to the northwest of Midway. Admiral Fletcher ordered Spruance to send the *Enterprise* and *Hornet* air groups to attack the enemy flattops as soon as their position had been fixed. Fletcher would follow as soon as he re-

The American carrier *Yorktown* was badly battered during the Battle of the Coral Sea and was hastily repaired in late May 1942 at Pearl Harbor. Admiral King wanted to send her back into the South Pacific, but Admiral Nimitz convinced him that all of the carriers would be needed in early June to defend the Hawaii-Midway axis.

covered search planes that had been launched by the *Yorktown*. Meanwhile, the Japanese had already launched seventy-two high-level and dive bombers, escorted by thirty-six Zeros; this group was headed toward Midway.

Every serviceable plane based on Midway was ordered to attack the Japanese carriers, while twenty-six Marine fighters, mostly outmoded Buffaloes, were kept in reserve to intercept the swarm of incoming bombers. In the ensuing attack, seventeen of the out-classed American fighters were shot down and installations on Midway were damaged. Nevertheless, with help from the heavy ground fire, the defenders downed a third of the attacking aircraft. The planes which had counterattacked Nagumo's carriers also suffered heavily, but without doing serious harm to the strongly defended Japanese fleet. One Japanese officer noted that the American torpedoes "didn't have any speed at all," and one was exploded by machine-gun fire as it porpoised.

So far, most of the honors had gone to the Japanese. But the decisive moment of the battle—and of the entire war in the Pacific —was at hand. Admiral Nagumo had kept ninety-three bombers armed with bombs and torpedoes in readiness on the flight decks of his carriers, and his cruisers had catapulted off several reconnaissance planes to look for the enemy fleet. Before the search planes reported back, the commander of the Midway bombing force suggested another attack be made on the atoll's defenses. Thus, at 0715 Nagumo ordered the torpedo planes spotted on his carrier's flight deck to be struck below and reloaded with bombs for a follow-up raid on Midway. But no sooner had the plane

Underway refueling, here of the *Lexington* in May 1942, was one of the major achievements of the U.S. Navy in the Pacific during the war.

handlers begun wrestling the loaded bombers down to the hangar deck so their cargoes could be changed, than a scout plane radioed that it had sighted ten enemy ships about 300 miles away. The vessels did not seem to be accompanied by carriers so the Admiral continued switching the payloads of his bombers. He did not learn that the enemy fleet was accompanied by a carrier until 0820 —when the planes had already been loaded for a ground strike.

Then, urged on by Commander Minoru Genda, his air operations officer, Nagumo ordered that the reserve planes be reloaded with torpedoes and armor-piercing bombs for a strike against ships. But before the reserve planes could be brought back up to the flight deck and flown off, the returning Midway strike force had to be recovered, refueled and rearmed. For the next hour, the flight decks of the Japanese carriers were crisscrossed with fuel lines. Ammunition, bombs and torpedoes were haphazardly strewn

A Lockheed PV-2 Harpoon twin-engine patrol bomber is loaded with a torpedo at an Aleutians base for strikes on Japanese shipping in the Kuriles in April 1942. The Harpoon was an enlarged and modified PV-1 Ventura with a range of over two thousand miles and a speed of greater than 300 mph.

A cannibalized F4F Wildcat fighter at Midway Island in June 1942.

about, as the deck crews struggled frantically to get their charges back into the air.

Meanwhile, pilots in the ready rooms of the *Hornet* and *Enterprise* joked nervously as they awaited word that the Japanese carriers had been sighted. They tried to brush aside the sobering thought that there would be empty seats in the wardroom that night. "Pilots, man your planes!" ordered the metallic voice on the squawk box. "Pilots, man your planes!" Taking advantage of the confusion on the Japanese carriers as they refueled and rearmed, Admiral Spruance had waited until this moment to launch his air groups. The strike consisted of sixty-seven SBD dive bombers and twenty-nine TBD torpedo planes, with an escort of twenty Wildcats. The *Yorktown* also put seventeen SBDs, a dozen TBDs and six fighters into the air.

The Japanese had changed course, however, and when the Americans arrived at the position where they expected to find the

TBD Devastators of Torpedo Squadron 6 on board the *Enterprise* before take-off on June 4, 1942. In heroic attacks against Japanese carriers that day, thirty-five of forty-one Devastators were destroyed. However, as Japanese fighters engaged in the low-altitude slaughter of the Devastators, American dive bombers remained undetected, and were thus able to deliver lethal blows to the Japanese carriers.

enemy, there was only empty sea. But a squadron of fifteen TBDs from the *Hornet*—Torpedo 8—found the carriers and, without fighter cover, they gallantly pressed home an attack. Before taking off, Lieutenant Commander John C. Waldron had told his squadron: "I want each of us to do his utmost to destroy our enemies. If there is only one plane left to make a final run in, I want that man to go in and get a hit. May God be with us all."[25]

Zeros and an antiaircraft barrage met the ungainly TBDs, and sent them splashing into the sea as if they had smashed into a stone wall. Only one man survived, Ensign George Gay. Although wounded, he fought his way to the surface after his plane sank and hid under his rubber seat cushion until the strafing Zeros had left. He was picked up by a PBY the next day. Two other squadrons of TBDs also attacked the carriers, only to be slaughtered by the alert combat air patrols. In all, only six of the forty-one torpedo planes survived this mission—and not a single torpedo had struck a Japanese ship.

But their sacrifice was not in vain. They diverted the attention of the Japanese fighter pilots and antiaircraft gunners from fifty-four approaching SBDs from the *Enterprise* and *Yorktown*. These swooped down on the *Akagi*, *Kaga* and *Soryu*, whose decks were still crowded with the planes being serviced. Lieutenant Clarence E. Dickinson, one of the dive-bomber pilots, reported:

As I put my nose down I picked up our carrier target in front of me. I was making the best dive I had ever made. . . . We were coming down in all directions on the port side of the carrier, beautifully spaced.

The Sichi D3A2 Val was the standard Japanese dive bomber during the early months of the Pacific War. With a speed of 242 mph, a range of 1,200 miles, and carrying one 551-pound bomb and two 130-pound bombs, the Val figured prominently in battles from Pearl Harbor to Santa Cruz. By mid-1943, most Vals had been lost along with their experienced pilots. In the background is the Japanese carrier *Kaga*.

During the Japanese diversionary attack on the Aleutians on the same day as the Battle of Midway, this Mitsubishi A6M2 Zero from the carrier *Ryujo* crashed on Akutan Island. Although the pilot was killed, the aircraft was captured intact and exhaustively flight-tested by the Americans.

A U.S. Navy PBY-5A Catalina long-range flying boat lands at Amchitka in the Aleutians. The large, ungainly-looking aircraft had a maximum range of 4,000 miles and a maximum speed just under 200 mph. The Catalina was the mainstay of U.S. naval long-range reconnaissance. A British Catalina also figured prominently in the hunt for the German battleship *Bismarck*.

Fire and damage to the island and flight deck of the *Yorktown* during the Battle of Midway, June 4, 1942.

. . . I recognized her as the *Kaga*; and she was enormous. . . . The target was utterly satisfying. . . . I saw a bomb hit just behind where I was aiming. . . . I saw the deck rippling and curling back in all directions exposing a great section of the hangar below. . . . I dropped a few seconds after the previous explosion. . . . I saw the 500-pound bomb hit right abreast of the island. The two 110-pound bombs struck in the forward area of the parked planes. . . . Then I began thinking it was time to get myself away from there. . . .[26]

Four bombs struck the *Kaga*, and the fires fed on ruptured fuel lines, touching off secondary explosions among her parked planes. Engulfed in soaring flames, she would finally sink that evening after being abandoned. The *Akagi* was hit by a bomb that ripped open her flight deck and another fell among the planes. She was turned into a flaming pyre, and as soon as Admiral Nagumo transferred his flag to a cruiser, she was sunk by escorting destroyers. The *Soryu* was hit by three 1,000-pound bombs and within twenty minutes, the entire vessel was blazing out of control.

Because of poor visibility, the fourth Japanese carrier, the *Hiryu*, had not been sighted by the SBDs. She was able to launch two waves, totaling forty dive-bombers, torpedo planes and fighters

On June 4, 1942, during the Battle of Midway, the carrier *Yorktown*'s island was damaged by an enemy bomb.

against the *Yorktown*. "Well, I've got on my tin hat," said Admiral Fletcher as he watched the approach of the enemy aircraft. "I can't do anything else now."[27] The *Yorktown*'s combat air patrol shot down many of the first wave of Japanese planes, but the carrier was also hit by three bombs, which started several serious fires. Damage-control parties succeeded in getting the *Yorktown* underway again, but just as most of her protecting Wildcats were being refueled, she was attacked by torpedo planes and hit twice. Listing badly and without power, she was abandoned, but refused to sink and was taken in tow.

Dive bombers from the *Enterprise* had already avenged the *Yorktown's* attack however. They had found the defenseless *Hiryu* —she had lost most of her fighters during the battle—and so badly battered her that she had to be scuttled. Thus, within a few hours, the Japanese had lost all four of their carriers, along with their crack air groups and about 250 planes. When the news reached

Sunk at the Battle of Midway in June 1942, the *Hiryu* had been the pride of the Japanese Navy when she entered the fleet in 1939. She displaced 16,000 tons, made 34 knots, and carried 55 warplanes. After Midway, the Japanese naval staff estimated that she could be replaced under their shipbuilding schedule no earlier than 1948!

95

Admiral Yamamoto on the *Yamato*'s bridge, "the members of the staff, their mouths shut tight, looked at one another," reported a witness.[28] Faced with the hard fact that the Americans still had two operational carriers while he had none, Yamamoto gave the order to withdraw. There was no pursuit, for rather than risking a night action against the big guns of the undamaged Japanese battleships, Admiral Spruance elected to turn away.

Two days later on June 6, American planes, which had been nipping at the heels of the retreating Japanese, caught up with the cruisers *Mogami* and *Mikuma*. The planes sunk the *Mikuma* and crippled the *Mogami;* the latter, however, somehow managed to make her way back to the Japanese base at Truk. Earlier that day, an enemy submarine had picked off the *Yorktown* and an accompanying destroyer. The next morning, with lowered colors and all hands at attention, the escort vessels paid final tribute to the carrier as she sank beneath the waves. The Battle of Midway was over.

Midway confirmed the vital role of the carrier in modern naval warfare. With a single thrust, Spruance and Fletcher had destroyed the offensive capability of a fleet with far stronger gunpower than their own—and inflicted upon the Imperial Japanese Navy its first decisive defeat since 1592. The flood tide of Japanese conquest had been halted in both the Coral Sea and the central Pacific, and Japan now faced the prolonged war that Yamamoto had warned against. Now the time had come for the U.S. Navy to shift to the offensive.

7

Guadalcanal

The American offensive in the Pacific began at first light on August 7, 1942. Slicing through the ominously dark waters of Savo Sound, an invasion fleet of some eighty vessels ranged off Guadalcanal and Tulagi in the southern Solomons. Over the loudspeakers came a command to be repeated often in coming years: "Land the landing force!" Protected by the guns of five American and three Australian cruisers, and by bombers and fighters flown off the *Saratoga, Enterprise* and *Wasp,* some 16,000 men of the First Marine Division splashed ashore. Resistance from the surprised Japanese was light and the invaders quickly secured the uncompleted airfield on Guadalcanal, key to control of the Solomons chain and the adjacent seas. But in the months to come, the swampy fever-ridden island and its surrounding waters were to become the scene of a fierce and bloody struggle.

Allied strategy called for the defeat of Germany—which had declared war on the United States on December 11, 1941—before subjugating Japan. But Admiral King had no intention of letting the Japanese consolidate their conquests. Using what limited resources could be diverted from a planned landing in North Africa, a step-by-step advance was to be launched up the Solomons and Bismarck Archipelago, until Rabaul, the center of Japanese strength in the Southwest Pacific, had been captured or neutralized. The first objective was Guadalcanal, on the northern fringe of the Coral Sea and some 560 nautical miles from Rabaul.

Rapidly recovering from their surprise at the landing, the Japanese lost no time in counterattacking. Twenty-seven Betty bombers escorted by eighteen Zeros headed south from Rabaul toward the invasion fleet, which lay just within their range. Two of the fighters were piloted by the Imperial Navy's top aces—Flight Petty Officer Saburo Sakai and Warrant Officer Hiroyoshi Nishizawa. The Bettys were followed by a flight of nine Val dive bombers which were on a one-way mission, because they lacked the fuel capacity to return to their base. Nearing Guadalcanal, the fighters split up into two groups, one group of nine, including Nishizawa, tangling with the Wildcats of the American combat air patrol. Withholding his fire until he was at point-blank range, Nishizawa shot down five planes before making his getaway. The other nine Zeros, including a section led by Sakai, accompanied the Bettys over the massed warships and transports, where they dropped their bombs without scoring any hits.

Turning for home, the Japanese planes were attacked by Wildcats and in the melee, several of the bombers were shot down. Sakai downed a Wildcat after a savage dogfight. Later, Sakai and a wingmate spotted a formation of eight enemy aircraft which he

An SBD Dauntless dive bomber of the *Enterprise* is loaded with a 500-pound demolition bomb for attacks against Japanese positions during the first day of American landings on Guadalcanal and Tulagi.

A pair of American SBD Dauntless dive bombers parked on the deck of the aircraft carrier *Yorktown* on July 24, 1942, two weeks before the Guadalcanal landings.

took for fighters. They attacked from astern, only to learn that the planes were new Grumman TBF Avenger torpedo bombers and their rear gunners were waiting for them. "The whole world exploded and the Zero rocked and shook like a toy," Sakai said later. "I felt as though I had been smashed on the head with a club."[29] Blinded in one eye and with a serious head wound, the groggy Sakai plummeted toward the sea. Revived by the rush of air through his shattered windshield, he managed to right his battered Zero and, despite several blackouts, made it back to Rabaul.

Meanwhile, the nine Val dive bombers attacked the invasion fleet. The destroyer *Mugford* was damaged, but all of the Vals were lost; six were shot down and three ran out of fuel. In all, the Japanese lost five Bettys and two Zeros as well as all nine of the Vals, while the American losses totaled eight Wildcats and an SBD. The Japanese attacked again on the following day, August

101

Japanese naval Betty bombers—flown without their bomb-bay doors—penetrated American antiaircraft fire in an attempt to assault invasion shipping off Guadalcanal on August 8, 1942.

Ensign W. M. Rouse, flying an F4F Wildcat off the large carrier *Enterprise*, shot down two Japanese torpedo bombers during the invasion of Guadalcanal from August 7 to 9, 1942.

8, sending in twenty-three Bettys, fitted with torpedoes this time, as well as another nine Vals and a fighter escort. Forewarned of the enemy's approach by Australian coastwatchers, Admiral Richmond Kelly Turner, commander of the amphibious forces, was ready for them. A swarm of Wildcats and heavy antiaircraft fire from the ships shot down eighteen of the Japanese planes. The destroyer *Jarvis* was torpedoed but was able to limp away, and a transport was set ablaze by a Japanese pilot who deliberately smashed into her.

The first American offensive of the war—and the first amphibious operation launched by the U.S. Navy since 1898—was proceeding according to timetable. "The results so far achieved make

On August 7, 1942, the Americans launched their "first offensive" in World War II—against the Japanese-held islands of Guadalcanal and Tulagi in the Lower Solomons. An opportunistic operation conceived to commit the United States to fighting in the Pacific before its armies engaged the European Axis in North Africa, the strategy was the brainchild of Chief of Naval Operations, Admiral Ernest J. King. In this photograph, SBD Dauntless dive bombers take off from the aircraft carrier *Wasp* on the first day of the invasion.

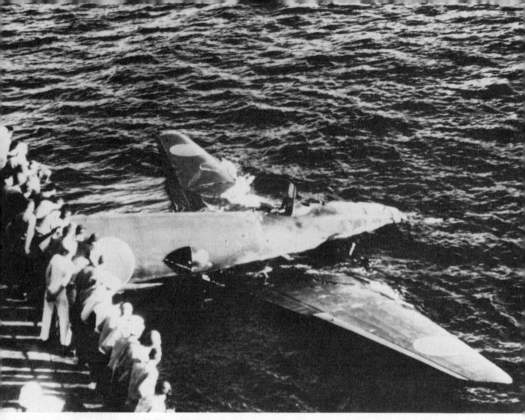

A Japanese Betty naval bomber floating off Tulagi after being shot down during air attacks on U.S. Navy forces, August 8, 1942. Designed for maximum range at all costs, the Betty was a lightly armored flying fuel tank, easily set afire by light damage. Later versions were greatly modified in an attempt to remedy this defect.

every officer and man in the South Pacific area proud of the task forces," declared Vice Admiral Robert L. Ghormley, the overall commander. But the Japanese had not given up. Vice Admiral Gunichi Mikawa hastily assembled a striking force of five heavy cruisers, including his flagship the *Chokai*, two light cruisers and a destroyer, and raced down from Rabaul. In a daring gamble, he steamed down the passage through the central Solomons—the "Slot"—in broad daylight so he could attack the Allied ships in Savo Sound in the early-morning darkness of August 9. Mikawa hoped to surprise the enemy and capitalize on the thorough training of his crews in night fighting.

Bad luck and blunders by his opponents greatly assisted him. Cooperation between the "black-shoe," or surface sailors, and the

104

airmen, or "brown-shoe" sailors, broke down. Admiral Fletcher chose this moment to withdraw his three carriers, much to the anger of Admiral Turner, who needed another day to get his transports unloaded. Despite Turner's protest, Ghormley approved the withdrawal. "He knew his situation in detail; I did not," Ghormley said later.[30] Fletcher claimed that his carriers needed refueling, but the real reason for his withdrawal was that he did not want to expose his carriers to attack. Fletcher had lost the *Lexington* and *Yorktown* in previous battles, and was evidently determined not to repeat the experience. Whatever the reason, his withdrawal left the beachhead and the fleet without air cover. To compound the problem, the reports of Australian reconnaissance planes that sighted Japanese ships in the Slot were delayed, incomplete, or misinterpreted. For example, two of Mikawa's cruisers were identified as seaplane tenders, creating the impression among the

On August 8, 1942, American naval aircraft attacked and damaged facilities at the Japanese seaplane base on the small island of Tanambogo, which was near Tulagi.

An F4F Wildcat takes off from the carrier *Enterprise* in the Coral Sea late in 1942.

Americans that the Japanese were planning an air attack, rather than a surface attack.

Early on the morning of August 9, the Japanese cruisers burst into Savo Sound at a speed of 26 knots. Before general quarters could be sounded, deadly Long Lance torpedoes were speeding toward the Allied ships, and they were engulfed by a rain of shells. In a few frenzied minutes, the American cruisers *Vincennes*, *Astoria* and *Quincy* and their Australian consort *Canberra* were sunk, and the *Chicago* was badly damaged. Two thousand men went down with their ships or were wounded. But Admiral Mikawa, not knowing that Fletcher had taken his carriers to sea, and wary of being attacked at any moment from the air, withdrew without striking at Turner's helpless transports. Almost before the Allies knew what had struck them, the Japanese forces had vanished. Coming on top of revelations about the inferiority of American fighters to the Zero and the ineffectiveness of American torpedoes, the Battle of Savo Island was a rude shock. It was, said

Samuel Eliot Morison, "probably the worst defeat ever inflicted on the United States Navy in a fair fight."

Since he was without air cover, Turner abandoned the beachhead on the evening of August 9, producing bitter comments from the Marines left behind to face a precarious future on Guadalcanal. As Major General Alexander A. Vandegrift, the Marine commander, pungently put it, they were left "bare ass." Until both sides began slipping in reinforcements about a week later, the island was left in limbo. Guadalcanal soon became a symbol to both sides, however. To the Americans it represented their determination to remain on the offensive; to the Japanese its loss would threaten the security of their newly conquered empire. Over the next six months, a half-dozen surface and air battles

An SBD dive bomber destroyed by a Japanese air raid on Henderson Field, Guadalcanal in August 1942. Strategy on both sides during the campaign was dubious. The Americans lost more men to malaria than to the enemy; they had no concept of where the operation might end or what they would do if the enemy contested the island. On the other hand, the Japanese decided to accept the American challenge and delivered forces piecemeal onto the island to be swallowed up by the Marines. In addition, the Japanese initiated an air war of attrition with the Americans, the one sort of campaign that they admitted to themselves that they could not win because of their industrial inferiority.

would be fought for control of this dreary speck of jungle. The adjacent body of water would become so littered with sunken ships that it was called Ironbottom Sound.

✻   ✻   ✻

On August 20, the escort carrier *Long Island,* a converted merchantman and the first vessel of its type in the U.S. Navy, launched two Marine squadrons of Wildcats and SBDs. The planes landed at Lunga Point on the north side of Guadalcanal, using the air strip which had been captured from the Japanese. Completed by Seabees, or men of the naval construction battalions, the strip was named Henderson Field in memory of Major Lofton Henderson, a Marine dive bomber pilot lost at Midway. Major John L. Smith, leader of the fighter squadron, scored Henderson Field's first kill, shooting down a Zero the day after his arrival. It was the first of the nineteen Japanese planes he bagged during the campaign.

Life at Henderson Field was grim. The air strip was either a sea of mud or a bowl of black dust that fouled engines and guns. Fuel was short and was fed into the planes with primitive hand pumps. Radio communications were difficult to maintain. The pilots of the "Cactus Air Force," as they called themselves, lived on a diet of Spam, dehydrated potatoes and captured rice. They flew all day, and efforts to sleep at night were often interrupted by Japanese float planes—"Louis the Louse" or "Washing Machine Charley"—that dropped a few random bombs, or by offshore shelling from Japanese warships. Most of the men developed malaria or dysentery, and some had both.

And there were the Zeros. Wildcat pilots tried to avoid dogfights with the faster and more maneuverable Japanese fighters, making the incoming Bettys their primary targets. Diving out of the sun, they aimed at the Bettys' unprotected wing tanks and set afire as many as they could. If a Zero got on a Wildcat's tail, the American could only hope that someone would pick it off. Very quickly the Marines adopted a defensive tactic known as the "Thach weave," developed earlier at Midway by Lieutenant Commander John S. Thach, a Navy fighter pilot, which proved effective against the Zero. They flew in two-pair, four-plane formations, which when attacked, turned inward on each other, giving the enemy pilot a difficult shot, and allowing each man as he swung about a crack at the Zero on a wingmate's tail. Captain

108

Shooting down four Japanese planes during the Guadalcanal landings and four more in the Battle of the Eastern Solomons, Machinist Donald E. Runyan proved that, in capable hands, the F4F Wildcat was the equal in combat of Japanese warplanes.

Joseph E. Foss was the high scorer among the "Cactus" Marines with twenty-six victories, and was awarded the Medal of Honor.

Ever since the debacle off Savo Island, Admiral Ghormley had expected the Japanese to return in force. On August 23, the "Tokyo Express"—a convoy of destroyers and fast transports with reinforcements for the hard-pressed Japanese garrison at Guadalcanal —came down from the main enemy base at Truk. With them were Admiral Nagumo's carriers, the *Zuikaku* and *Shokaku* and the smaller *Ryujo*, and the battleships *Hiei* and *Kirishima*. Admiral Fletcher was ordered up from Nouméa with the *Saratoga*, *Enterprise* and *Wasp* and the new battleship *North Carolina*. SBDs and TBFs from the *Saratoga* joined the Henderson Field Marines in searching for the enemy ships. When this attempt failed, Fletcher, convinced that the Japanese were still several days' steaming away, detached the *Wasp* for refueling. The American fleet was thus deprived of one-third of its carrier strength when the Battle of the Eastern Solomons erupted on the following morning, August 24.

The Japanese opened up with an attack on Henderson Field by bombers and fighters from the *Ryujo* which were joined over Guadalcanal by twin-engine bombers that had flown in from Rabaul. They were jumped by the Cactus Air Force, which downed twenty-one of the attacking aircraft. Captain Marion E. Carl shot down two bombers and a Zero; he ran his total score to 18½ planes by the campaign's end. In the meantime, the *Ryujo* had been sighted and Fletcher ordered a strike against her by thirty SBDs and six TBFs. Penetrating heavy flak and evading the defending Zeros, they hit her with at least ten bombs and one torpedo. She began burning fiercely, and was abandoned by her crew. None of the American planes were lost.

The Japanese had spotted the *Enterprise* and *Saratoga,* and Nagumo must have congratulated himself on the opportunity to hit them while their planes were attacking the unlucky *Ryujo.* But Fletcher was ready. Having learned the lesson of Midway, he had increased his combat air patrols until there were fifty-three Wildcats in the air, and the flight decks of his ships had been cleared of planes. The two air armadas collided about twenty-five miles from the *Enterprise* and in the wild melee Warrant Machinist Donald E. Runyan downed two Val dive bombers and a Zero, and damaged a third Val. Even the SBDs and TBFs returning from the strike against the *Ryujo* joined in the battle, shooting down three more Vals.

Two dozen Vals cut their way through to the *Enterprise,* and as they dived on her, the carrier was forced to rely for protection upon her guns and those of the *North Carolina* and the other ships in her screen. The sky was filled with globs of black smoke from exploding shells and the tracers burned through the sky. Several dive bombers were blown to bits by direct hits and another two or three that had been damaged tried to crash into the carrier. One officer became so excited that he emptied his .45-caliber pistol at the raiders. The *Enterprise*'s skipper, Captain Arthur C. Davis, noted that the attack was carried out with precision, the Vals diving at seven-second intervals. In little more than four minutes, the attack was over. The *Enterprise* had been hit by three bombs, one of which crashed through her flight deck to explode in the crew's quarters, killing thirty men. Another thirty-nine men were wiped out by a bomb that fell on the starboard gun gallery. The "Big E" was swept by flames, but her damage-control and firefighting crews performed magnificently, and within an hour she resumed flight operations.

The battle ended indecisively. The American planes did not find the *Shokaku* and *Zuikaku*, and a second wave of Japanese bombers also failed to find their targets. Two SBDs from the *Saratoga* which had gotten separated from the main strike force attacked the seaplane carrier *Chitose*, thinking that she was a battleship, and heavily damaged her. The following morning, eight SBDs from Henderson Field found the "Tokyo Express" itself. They pummeled the escorting cruiser *Jintsu* and set ablaze a large transport. Although eight B-17s appeared as the destroyer *Mutsuki* stood by to take off the stricken vessel's troops and crew, her captain, Commander K. Hatano, disdainful of the degree of accuracy heretofore shown by the high-level bombers, went ahead with his work. Three bombs quickly sank his ship. "Even the B-17s could make a hit once in a while," he grumbled, after being pulled from the sea.[31]

The Battle of the Eastern Solomons was an American victory, for the Japanese had lost the *Ryujo* and a significant number of planes, and had been prevented from landing reinforcements. "Our plan to capture Guadalcanal came unavoidably to a standstill," a Japanese officer commented. Nevertheless, there were serious defects in American operations. Search planes had failed to find the *Shokaku* and *Zuikaku*, and only luck had prevented the Japanese from launching another strike which might have been fatal to the *Enterprise* and *Saratoga*.

* * *

Over the next two months both sides augmented their forces on Guadalcanal. Under the cover of aircraft from the carriers and Henderson Field, the Americans sent in a constant stream of cargo vessels. Although Japanese bombers from Rabaul continued to pound the island, enemy submarines were the greatest peril faced by the Americans. The eastern approaches to the Coral Sea became known as "Torpedo Junction." On August 30, the *Saratoga*

In the center, Admiral William F. Halsey, Jr., Commander of the South Pacific Area—later, Commander of the Fifth Fleet. The newspapers nicknamed him "Bull," an appropriate and affectionate title. An aviator, Halsey was profane, aggressive, rash, impulsive, likeable, an indifferent administrator, and sincere.

was torpedoed, and because the dockyard at Pearl Harbor was crowded with damaged ships, she had to go all the way to the West Coast for repairs. Two weeks later the *Wasp* caught fire after being hit by three torpedoes, and had to be abandoned. The *North Carolina* was also damaged at the same time. Following these disasters, the *Hornet* was the U.S. Navy's only operational carrier in the Pacific. The "Tokyo Express" continued its nightly runs of men and supplies to Japanese-held beaches, shelling American positions and then scooting to safety. On one occasion, two battleships pounded Henderson Field, sending its supply of aviation fuel up in flames, smashing the landing strip and destroying forty-eight planes. By the end of the month, the Japanese had landed some 20,000 men on Guadalcanal.

Vice Admiral Thomas C. Kinkaid

"It now appears that we are unable to control the sea in the Guadalcanal area," said Admiral Nimitz in a grim survey of the situation. "Thus our supply of the positions will only be done at great expense to us. This situation is not hopeless, but it is certainly critical."[32] To deal with the problem, Nimitz named Admiral Halsey, now healthy and eager for action, to replace Ghormley as overall commander of naval forces in the South Pacific, while Rear Admiral Thomas C. Kinkaid took over control of carrier operations from Fletcher. Halsey's appointment had an electrifying effect upon his new command. "I'll never forget it," said an officer. "One minute we were too limp with malaria to crawl out of our fox-holes; the next we were running around whooping like kids."[33] In Washington, Admiral King persuaded President Roosevelt to put more men, planes and ships into the Southwest Pacific campaign.

Admiral Yamamoto, believing that the Americans were now on the ropes, gathered his forces for a knockout punch. The Japanese launched a massive land offensive against the Marine defenders of Henderson Field, while a striking force of five battleships and four carriers—the *Shokaku, Zuikaku, Zuiho* and *Junyo,* again under Admiral Nagumo—cruised to the northeast of the Santa Cruz Islands. Yamamoto's orders to his subordinates were succinct: "Apprehend and annihilate any powerful forces in the Solomons area, as well as any reinforcements." Halsey accepted the challenge and sent the *Hornet* and the hastily repaired *Enterprise* into the fray, along with the new battleship *South Dakota,* which had been fitted with dozens of Bofors 40-mm antiaircraft guns in twin and quadruple mounts. "Attack—Repeat—Attack!" Halsey radioed his commanders at dawn on October 26, upon receiving word from a prowling PBY that the Japanese were in the area.

Kinkaid launched sixteen SBDs from the *Enterprise* on a search and attack mission and they scoured the sea in pairs. Lieutenant Commander James R. Lee and his wingmate, Ensign William E. Johnson, found the enemy ships about 185 miles away, but before they could attack, eight Zeros jumped them. They managed to shoot down three of the fighters and make good their escape. Two other dive bombers, piloted by Lieutenant Stockton B. Strong and Ensign Charles B. Irvine, evaded the combat air patrol and attacked the *Zuiho,* smallest of the enemy carriers. One of their 500-

"Mail call" for personnel of VB 106 at an airfield in the Southwest Pacific.

pound bombs opened a gaping hole in the *Zuiho*'s flight deck and set her afire. Unable to recover her planes, she limped away to Truk. By then, the Japanese had pinpointed the American carriers and 135 bombers and fighters sped toward the target. They passed 73 American aircraft heading in the opposite direction and shot down eight of them in the ensuing dogfight.

Coming in at 17,000 feet, the Japanese broke through the defending fighters and with the *Enterprise* hidden by a rain squall,

A Navy PB4Y Liberator long-range patrol bomber takes off on a photo-reconnaissance mission from Guadalcanal in 1943. Nine hundred PB4Y aircraft served in naval units during the war.

concentrated on the *Hornet*. Twenty-five of the attacking planes were shot down by the heavy barrage of antiaircraft fire thrown up by the carrier and her screen. But the *Hornet* was hit several times. A Val that had been damaged by flak crashed into her flight deck, setting her afire. Two torpedoes also smashed into the stricken carrier's engine room and she stopped dead in the water. The Japanese now turned their attention to the "Big E" which had emerged from the mist, but because of the effectiveness of American defensive fire only scored two minor hits upon her. Several of her escorts were damaged, however, including the *South Dakota*, and a destroyer was sunk by a submarine. An attempt was made to tow the *Hornet* out of the battle zone but she was struck again and again by enemy planes. With darkness falling, the blazing flattop was abandoned and left to be sunk by Japanese destroyers.

In the meantime, the *Hornet*'s planes reached the *Shokaku*. With Zeros on their tails, the SBDs nosed down into their dives and planted four 1,000-pound bombs on her flight deck. Unfortunately, the accompanying TBFs had become separated and did not locate the crippled Japanese flattop, for a well-placed torpedo or two might well have finished her off. As it was, nine months were

116

Aircrewmen pose near the nose of their PB4Y-1 Unapproachable on an airfield in the South Pacific, in 1943–44.

THIS BOOK PROPERTY OF
STANLEY J. BLAZEWSKI
519 W 2ND AV ROSSELLE NJ

needed to again make her operational. The cruiser *Chikuma* was also severely battered. The *Enterprise* strike force, disorganized by the Japanese fighters which had attacked them on the way to their targets, were almost out of fuel by the time they found the enemy ships, and the attacks launched were ineffectual.

The Battle of the Santa Cruz Islands was a tactical victory for the Japanese. They had sunk a carrier and damaged a battleship, while sustaining damage to two carriers. But Yamamoto was unable to exploit his advantage. He had lost more than 100 planes to the deadly fire of the new antiaircraft guns carried by the American ships, and his corps of experienced air crews was greatly reduced. Santa Cruz was to be the last decisive Japanese victory of the war.

Realizing that Henderson Field was the key to victory, Yamamoto decided to land more troops on Guadalcanal to capture the strip. In the dark hours of the morning of November 13—a Friday —the "Tokyo Express," led by the battleships *Hiei* and *Kirishima*, came down the Slot to shell Henderson Field so that its planes would be unable to interfere with the eleven heavily laden transports that were following. An American cruiser and destroyer force gave battle, and by the time daylight came, the heavily damaged *Hiei* was turning in circles off Savo Island. Dive bombers and torpedo planes from Henderson Field and the *Enterprise*, back at sea despite an unrepaired flight deck elevator, finished her off. She was the first Japanese battleship sunk during the war.

Undeterred, the Japanese pressed ahead with plans to reinforce their troops on Guadalcanal, but American carrier- and land-based aircraft sank all but four of the transports. The American triumph was augmented on the night of November 14 when the big guns of the battleships *Washington* and *South Dakota* battered the *Kirishima* so badly that she was scuttled by her crew. Even though the U.S. Navy continued to suffer serious losses, the American position on Guadalcanal was never threatened again. Early in the following year, the Japanese began evacuating the 11,000 nearly starving survivors of the some 30,000 men that had been landed on the island. On February 9, 1943, six months after the Marines had landed, General Alexander M. Patch signaled Halsey: "Tokyo Express no longer has terminus on Guadalcanal."

8

Victory in the Atlantic

Buffeted by strong winds, six torpedo-laden Swordfish slowly circled over the gray waters of the English Channel shortly after midday on February 12, 1942. Lieutenant Commander Eugene Esmonde, the flight leader, anxiously scanned the overcast sky looking for a promised escort of five squadrons of Spitfires and Hurricanes. Fifteen hundred feet below, the German battle cruisers *Scharnhorst* and *Gneisenau* and the cruiser *Prinz Eugen* were racing up the Channel, under an umbrella of some 300 Messerschmitt and Focke-Wulf fighters. As each minute passed, the enemy warships drew further away to the safety of a German port. A flock of Spitfires finally appeared but Esmonde's feeling of relief was brief, for he counted only ten British planes. Without adequate fighter cover, Esmonde realized that the odds against a successful attack were overwhelming. Nevertheless, he unhesitatingly led his Swordfish into battle.

The *Scharnhorst* and *Gneisenau* had been lying at Brest since the previous March, when they had returned from a raid into the Atlantic in which they had sunk more than 100,000 tons of Allied shipping. Not long afterward, they were joined by the *Prinz Eugen*, which had survived her ill-fated sortie with the *Bismarck*. There they remained, blockaded by sea and vulnerable to enemy bombers, but still an ever-present threat to Britain's maritime lifeline. Early in 1942, Adolf Hitler, convinced that the British were about to invade Norway, ordered a daring dash through the English Channel to home waters and thence to Norway. The powerful *Tirpitz*, sistership of the *Bismarck*, had already been sent to Trondheim to deal with the expected British assault.

Vice Admiral Otto Ciliax laid careful plans for the break-out.

In 1941, the British had bottled up the German battleships *Scharnhorst* (left) and *Gneisenau* (right), along with the heavy cruiser *Prinz Eugen,* in the occupied French port of Brest. In the late evening of February 11, 1942, they broke out, on Hitler's direct orders, and dashed up the Channel to join the battleship *Tirpitz* in Norway, where he hoped they could disrupt the Anglo-American convoys to Russia.

Rumors were spread that the ships were to make a sortie into the Atlantic. Meanwhile the proposed inshore route was swept of mines and a screen of destroyers and motor torpedo boats was provided, along with overwhelming air support. When the ships slipped out of Brest on the moonless night of February 11, the secret of their destination had been so well kept that even the crews believed they were taking part in another drill.

The British were caught flatfooted. Although the Admiralty had

Lieutenant Commander Eugene Esmonde, second from left, leader of the Swordfish attack on the *Scharnhorst* and *Gneisenau*.

expected the Germans to make a run through the Channel, the preparations were haphazard. No capital ships were sent into the area because of the danger of attack by the Luftwaffe, and the R.A.F. had been given the task of dealing with the threat. Early in February, 300 bombers were placed on two hours readiness. But when the Germans failed to come, two-thirds of the bombers were reassigned and the remainder were placed on four hours readiness—without the navy being informed. The British did not realize that the Germans were at sea until nearly noon of February 12, because of poor luck and a series of operational mishaps. By then the German ships had covered nearly two-thirds of their escape route and were almost off Dover. British forces were thrown piecemeal into the attack; first a handful of motor torpedo boats which were brushed aside, and then the half-dozen Fleet Air Arm Swordfish.

Esmonde and his seventeen pilots, gunners and observers had volunteered for a night attack on the German ships—a forlorn hope even under the best of circumstances. Now, with no warning, they were being asked to do the impossible. Under no illusions about

Esmonde's Swordfish making their runs on the *Scharnhorst* and *Gneisenau*. Photograph taken from one of the German ships.

An Arado 196 being catapulted from the German heavy cruiser *Prinz Eugen*. The 174-mph Arado 196 had a flight endurance of 3½ hours, and performed reconnaissance, gun-ranging observation, and submarine-chasing duties for the larger German warships.

the chance for success, Esmonde, a veteran of the attack on the *Bismarck,* agreed to make an attack in broad daylight when the R.A.F. promised an escort of five squadrons of fighters. "For the love of God," he pleaded with his superiors, "get the fighters to us on time."[34]

But most of the fighter squadrons failed to appear at the rendezvous because of poor weather. Esmonde decided there was no time to wait, because the German vessels were now off Ramsgate, an ideal place for an attack. The Swordfish pointed their noses down toward the sea while the ten Spitfires weaved back and forth above them. The German fighters jumped them well before they reached the ships, some tying the defending Spitfires up in dogfights while others blazed away at the torpedo planes. The slow-moving Swordfish were surprisingly elusive targets. Time and again, the Messerschmitts and Focke-Wulfs misjudged their speed and overshot them. When tracer bullets set Esmonde's plane afire, his gunner, Leading Airman W. J. Clinton, climbed out of the cockpit and sitting astride the fuselage, put out the flames with his gloved hands. He then calmly climbed back behind his gun.

All six of the Swordfish were eventually shot down, however, and their sacrifice was in vain for none of their torpedoes struck the speeding warships. Running the gauntlet of attacks by R.A.F. bombers and Royal Navy surface ships, the German ships reached the safety of the Elbe, although the *Scharnhorst* was damaged by two mines. Yet, as the head of the German Navy Grand Admiral Erich Raeder later acknowledged, the episode, although it appeared at the time to be a tactical success, was in reality a strategic defeat. Effectively bottled up in German ports, the vessels were no longer a threat to Allied shipping in the Atlantic. And their careers as fighting ships were soon over. The *Scharnhorst* was sunk by the British Home Fleet off North Cape in December 1943; the *Gneisnau* was so badly battered by R.A.F. bombers while in port that she never sailed again; and the *Prinz Eugen* was torpedoed by a British submarine which blew off her stern. She survived to become one of the target ships at the atomic bomb test at Bikini. Each of the Swordfish airmen who had participated in the gallant attack on the warships was decorated, fifteen of the awards made posthumously. Eugene Esmonde, whose body was washed up on the Kentish coat two months later, was awarded the Victoria Cross.

In the summer of 1942, Malta again faced a crisis. Bombed every day by German and Italian aircraft, the island fortress was on the brink of starvation and surrender. There was a deadly parallel between the state of its fortunes and the land campaign in North Africa. When Malta was well-supplied, aircraft based at its fields disrupted the Afrika Korps' supply lines across the Mediterranean; when Malta was weak, the Axis armies were on the move. Now, General Erwin Rommel's troops were on the verge of capturing the Suez Canal, and the entire Middle East, along with its vital oil fields, was in danger of falling into German hands.

On August 10, fourteen hastily gathered merchantmen, including the tanker *Ohio*, passed through the Straits of Gibraltar in a

The German heavy cruiser *Prinz Eugen* had quick-firing 8-inch guns which scored the first hit on the British battleship *Hood* before the *Bismarck*'s fatal salvo. Successfully escaping the *Bismarck*'s subsequent fate, *Prinz Eugen* led a charmed life throughout the war. Despite repeated damage, it was not until after being hit by an atom bomb during an experiment at Bikini Atoll in 1946 that the sturdy cruiser finally sank!

The Axis was defeated by American industrial capacity, which fed the Russians and the British with the goods of war, and which armed its own countrymen with the finest mass-produced weapons of the naval war. In this photograph, Army Air Force P-47-D5 fighters have been jammed onto the flight deck of the escort carrier *Block Island* at New York in July 1943, awaiting shipment to Europe.

desperate attempt to relieve Malta. The perceived value of the convoy—known as Pedestal—can be gauged by the strength of the escort. It included the modern carriers *Victorious* and *Indomitable* as well as the old *Eagle*, the battleships *Nelson* and *Rodney*, and a strong cruiser-destroyer screen. The *Furious* was also to accompany the convoy to a point 550 miles west of the island and fly off thirty-eight Spitfires that were badly needed by the R.A.F. Pedestal faced formidable odds. The Germans and Italians had massed nearly 800 aircraft in Sardinia and Italy, while twenty submarines and a sizable force of cruisers, destroyers and motor-torpedo boats had been thrown across its course.

127

Several enemy reconnaissance planes were seen, some of which were shot down by Hurricanes, but all was comparatively quiet until the mid-afternoon of August 11. Suddenly the convoy was rocked by a series of dull explosions. "Oh Christ! Look at the *Eagle*," someone cried out.[35] Four torpedoes fired by the *U-73* had nearly blown the old carrier apart, and she sank within eight minutes with a loss of some 200 of her crew. But there were no further attacks, and shortly before sunset the *Furious* launched her cargo of Spitfires and returned to Gibraltar.

An ominous silence descended upon the convoy, soon broken by the command, "Fighters stand-to!" Thirty-five Junkers 88s tried to bomb the ships but were driven off by Hurricanes and heavy antiaircraft fire. "The sight took our breath away," said Lieutenant Hugh Popham, one of the fighter pilots. "The light was slowly dying, and the ships were no more than a pattern on the great steel plate of the sea; . . . Every gun in the fleet was firing and the darkling air was laced with threads and beads of fire."[36]

In April 1942, the U. S. Navy lent the new battleship *Washington* to the Admiralty in order to release forces from the Home Fleet to substitute for units at Gibraltar which were assigned to seize French-held Madagascar. In this photograph, the *Washington* sits in Scapa Flow harbor with a British aircraft carrier in the background. The *Washington* escorted several convoys carrying Lend-Lease material to Russia on the Murmansk run, once narrowly missing an engagement with the German battleship *Tirpitz*.

Torpedoes being loaded on Junkers JU 88s for use against Allied shipping in the Mediterranean.

The Germans and Italians launched a major effort against the convoy as it neared Sardinia on the morning of August 12. More than a hundred aircraft of various types, accompanied by a strong escort, flew to the attack and were met by every fighter that could be launched by the flattops. Eleven German dive bombers broke through the fighter screen and so badly damaged a freighter that she had to be left behind. Mistaken for Hurricanes by the ships' harassed gunners, two Italian Reggiane 2000 fighter-bombers were allowed to drop a pair of bombs on the *Victorious*. One failed to explode; the other bounced off her armored flight deck into the sea. The Italians also used a primitive version of the guided missile: a pilotless aircraft packed with explosives that was guided by remote control from an accompanying plane. It droned harmlessly away over the horizon to crash into the North African desert.

The convoy was under continual attack for the rest of the day. The *Indomitable's* flight deck was damaged by German dive-

The troop transports *Orizaba* and *Joseph T. Dickman* steamed with the small aircraft carrier *Ranger,* enroute to Capetown, South Africa in November 1941, before the United States had formally entered the war. The tail section is from a Vought SB2U Vindicator bomber.

bombers but at nightfall the convoy was still more or less intact. When the last of the raiders had been beaten off, the *Victorious* and *Indomitable,* their task completed, bade farewell to the convoy and returned as scheduled to Gibraltar, as the convoy entered the narrow passage between Sicily and the North African coast. The fact that Pedestal had gotten so far with only minor losses was vivid testimony to the value of the air defense provided by the carriers.

The rest of the voyage was to be more difficult, however. The R.A.F. could provide little cover, and the convoy was attacked by wave after wave of bombers and torpedo planes, as well as submarines and torpedo boats. Two of the escorting cruisers were sunk and another pair damaged. Only five of the merchantmen survived the savage onslaught to arrive in the Grand Harbor of

130

Malta; but among them was the *Ohio* with her 15,000 precious tons of oil.

Partially resupplied and refueled, submarines and strike aircraft based on Malta played havoc with German and Italian shipments to North Africa. In August, 25 percent of Rommel's supplies were lost on the short and dangerous passage; by October, 44 percent of the total tonnage was being sunk. Little more than a month later, the Afrika Korps, short of ammunition and fuel, was reeling back across the North African desert in full retreat from El Alamein. As one British officer said, "the war in the desert was won on the airfields of Malta."

Two weeks before the British began their drive westward from Egypt, the Allies had landed in French North Africa, trapping Rommel between the two advancing armies. Operation Torch, first step on the long road back to the European mainland, was covered by the largest concentration of naval air power yet seen. No less than twelve American and British carriers, among them six escort carriers (CVEs), took part in the invasion. Built upon tanker and freighter hulls, the CVEs took part in naval operations in every theatre. More than 100 were turned out by American yards for both the British and American navies. They were not designed for operations against enemy fleets but proved invaluable for antisubmarine work, tactical air support, ferrying planes to land bases, and training.

The U.S. Navy's *Ranger* and four escort carriers, the *Sangamon, Chenango, Suwannee* and *Santee*, were assigned to the capture of Casablanca and Port Lyautey on the Atlantic coast of Morocco. The *Furious* and the British escort carriers *Biter* and *Dasher* covered the landings at Oran while the *Argus* and the escort carrier *Avenger* participated in the attack on Algiers. The *Victorious* and *Formidable* operated offshore with Force H, to prevent the Italian fleet from interfering with the invasion. The carriers could launch a total of about 400 planes, including the newly introduced Seafire, a Spitfire modified for carrier operations. The French had nearly 500 aircraft, and no one knew if they would oppose the landing. It was also feared that the Luftwaffe might take over the French airfields once the attack had begun.

Wildcats from the *Ranger* and the "jeep" carriers swept in over Casablanca at daylight on November 8, 1942, to strafe French air-

An American destroyer of pre-war design passes astern of the *Ranger* at sunset on November 8, 1942, the first day of the Torch landings on North Africa.

Two covering elements for the invasion of North Africa—the fifteen 6-inch guns of the light cruiser *Brooklyn*, and the thirty-four aircraft of the new escort carrier *Suwannee*.

fields and shore batteries. They destroyed twenty-one planes on the ground without loss to themselves. Later, a squadron of Wildcats tangled with sixteen French fighters, shooting down eight planes and wrecking another fourteen on the ground. Four Wildcats failed to return from this mission. Eighteen SBDs bombed enemy warships, antiaircraft batteries, and harbor installations. Old biwing Seagull observation planes catapulted off the battleship *Massachusetts* and a cruiser also played a unique role in the invasion when they halted a French tank column by dropping depth charges fitted with impact fuses. Two days later, nine SBDs, each carrying a 1,000-pound bomb, attacked the immobilized battleship *Jean Bart,* which had opened up on the cruiser *Augusta* with her remaining three 15-inch guns. Three hits were made, putting the vessel out of action. "No more *Jean Bart!*" radioed one of the jubilant pilots.[37]

The landings at Oran and Algiers encountered little resistance. Within a few hours of the capitulation of the French at Algiers, Spitfires and Hurricanes from Gibraltar were already using the base. Thus, with only slight losses in men, ships and planes, the Allies had effected three major landings in North Africa and had

Crewmen scrape paint as a fire-prevention measure in the American carrier *Ranger* while enroute to North Africa in November 1942. Experience during the first days of the Pacific war demonstrated the fire hazards of third coats of paint, built up by industrious seamen during the interwar years.

Wildcats test-fire machine guns aboard the *Ranger* prior to the North African landings. The oversize stars were painted to ensure that any possible French opposition would be well aware that the planes were American.

closed the trap on Rommel. German resistance on the southern shore of the Mediterranean finally ended on May 13, 1943.

The long arm of naval aviation was also called into play when the Allies launched an invasion of Europe on September 9. Because of the distance from newly captured airfields in Sicily to the beachhead at Salerno on the Italian mainland, land-based fighters could spend only twenty minutes over the battle zone. Thus the initial phase of the landing was protected by about a hundred Seafires from four British escort carriers. It was expected that this umbrella would be required only for a short time, since the nearby Montecorvino airfield was to be captured on the first day of the landing. But German resistance was fierce and for a

Commander of Task Group 34.2, Rear Admiral Ernest D. McWhater, and his chief of staff Captain John M. Ballantine, on the flag bridge of the *Ranger* enroute to North Africa prior to Operation Torch.

An American Douglas SBD scout plane from the *Ranger* flies antisubmarine patrols over the Torch invasion convoy enroute to North Africa in November 1942.

During the Torch invasion of North Africa in November 1942, Curtiss SOC-3 Seagulls were catapulted from the cruiser *Augusta* to observe bombardments ashore. Seagulls also served as scout planes for PT-boat night operations in the Solomons in the Pacific, and some even saw service as late as 1944.

time it looked as if the invading army would be thrown back into the sea. The Seafires were forced to continue operations for another two and a half days, until American engineers managed to carve out a rough airstrip to accommodate the first of the land-based fighters. By then only about twenty-five of the carrier fighters were still operational. Forty of them had been written off due to accidents resulting from the Seafires' weak landing gear; another ten had been lost to enemy fighters and flak.

Italy surrendered on the day of the Salerno invasion. With the Italian fleet immobilized and the Germans driven from the air, the

136

carriers were withdrawn. Naval aviation had played a paramount role in turning the Mediterranean into an Allied lake.

The German submarine campaign against Allied shipping in the Atlantic reached its greatest effectiveness in March 1943. Upwards of 567,000 tons of Allied shipping was sunk against the loss of only six U-boats. Although land-based aircraft provided cover for convoys at both ends of the voyage, there was a 600-mile-wide gap in the mid-Atlantic, beyond the range of such aircraft, that was known with good reason as the "Black Pit." Lacking air support, the escorting vessels were sometimes overwhelmed by the U-boats. Convoys would escape from one wolf pack only to be attacked by another. "The Germans never came so near to disrupting communications between the Old World and the New as in

The destroyer-minesweeper *Howard,* converted World War I-era, flush-deck destroyer, refuels underway from the escort carrier *Chenango,* enroute to Casablanca on November 29, 1942. Underway refueling extended the range of the fleet enormously—as well as lengthening the time on station—and significantly contributed to the U.S. Navy's "long legs."

An F4F Wildcat is launched from the *Ranger* to attack targets ashore during the Torch invasion. The first American ship built from the keel up as an aircraft carrier, the 14,500-ton *Ranger* was considered too small for operations in the Pacific and spent the years following the Torch invasion in training and antisubmarine missions in the Atlantic.

the first twenty days of March 1943," reported the Admiralty. And then, Admiral Karl Dönitz, the new Commander-in-Chief of the German Navy, took note of a development that marked the turn of the tide in the Battle of the Atlantic. "On March 26 an aircraft carrier was observed inside the screen of a westbound convoy," he said. "Its aircraft foiled the attempts of the U-boats to close the convoy."[38]

Four escort carriers, the U.S. Navy's *Bogue* and the British *Archer*, *Biter* and *Dasher*, became operational that month. They achieved nothing spectacular, but their TBFs and Swordfish, fitted with depth charges, prevented U-boats from attacking their convoys. As more ships became available, several specially-trained "hunter-killer" groups were organized with escort carriers at their

ATLANTIC AREA

An artist's depiction of a PB4Y Liberator's successful destruction of a German submarine in the Bay of Biscay. Adequate numbers of long-range patrol craft such as the PB4Y were important in limiting effective U-boat operations to the distant mid-Atlantic.

Sailors aboard the *Ranger* "stripping ship" in anticipation of action off Morocco, in early November 1942.

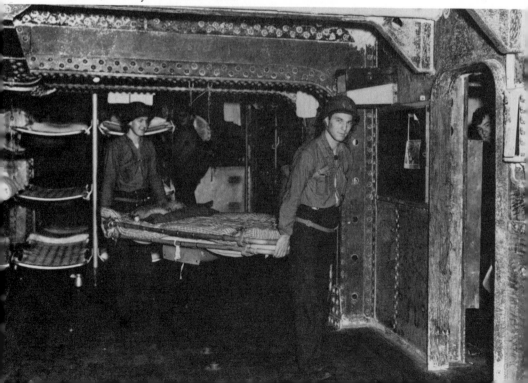

A non-rigid patrol airship, 251 feet long, on convoy duty in the Western Atlantic. Capable of carrying 1,200 lbs. of bombs or depth charges, the "blimps" had a range of over 2,000 miles at a cruising speed of 40 mph. Cheap and dependable, they were useful in antisubmarine operations during the war, but forsaken thereafter.

core. They were free to pursue submarine contacts without fear of leaving the convoy open to attack from other U-boats. The *Biter*, which was supporting a westbound convoy, became the first of these vessels to be credited with sinking a U-boat when her aircraft joined with a destroyer in making the kill on April 23, 1943. The *Archer* and *Bogue* also were soon credited with sinking submarines. And for every kill, other U-boats were driven off or damaged.

Increasing numbers of B-24 Liberator bombers also joined in providing continuous air cover over the North Atlantic convoys. Alerted by electronic intercepts of the considerable radio traffic between the U-boats and Dönitz's headquarters that, unknown to the Germans, was being decoded, Allied ships and planes reaped a harvest of submarines. In May alone, no less than forty-one German submarines failed to return from combat patrol. The Battle of the Atlantic had been won.

One of fifty mass-produced 7,800-ton escort carriers of the *Casablanca* class, the *Guadalcanal* earned fame with her capture of the German submarine *U-505*, the first foreign prize captured on the high seas by a U.S. Navy vessel since the War of 1812. The seizure, which occurred in June 1944 off the coast of West Africa, provided the Allies with valuable material useful in reading the German ULTRA codes.

Admiral King argued that only escorted convoys could defeat the U-boat and defeat the German threat of sea denial. In this photograph, a typical convoy gathers in Boston prior to making the treacherous transatlantic crossing in August 1942.

By the end of 1943, the main sea lines of communication in the North Atlantic were defended by task forces of escort carriers, such as the *Card*, destroyers, and destroyer escorts. On December 10, the *Card* retired into her home port to receive a presidential citation after sinking three U-boats. She had been directed to the German submarines by radio intelligence, which disclosed both the course and speed of the U-boats to their Allied predators.

Admiral Dönitz ordered his U-boats into southern waters, where another air "gap" existed, with the hope of picking off ships carrying supplies for the impending invasions of Sicily and Italy. The U.S. Navy's "hunter-killer" groups were ready for them. In one two-month period, the *Bogue, Card, Core* and *Santee* CVE groups sank thirteen submarines. On October 4, 1943, one of the *Card*'s planes attacked three U-boats being resupplied by a large "milch cow" submarine. The "milch cow" was sunk and the other three boats were damaged. One was sunk later in the day by another *Card* aircraft. In all, the *Bogue* accounted for ten U-boats while the *Card* had eight kills. Patrol planes and escort carriers of the Fourth Fleet, operating from the hump of Brazil, also played an important role in turning back the U-boat offensive in the South Atlantic.

A few of these battles recalled the single-ship duels of the age of fighting sail. In June 1944, the *Guadalcanal* group, commanded by Captain Daniel V. Gallery, forced the *U-505* to the surface and a boarding party swarmed on board before she could be scuttled.

143

Anchored in an English port, the British escort carrier *Battler* was built at the Ingalls shipyard in Pascagoula, Mississippi, and transferred to the Admiralty under the Lend-Lease program in 1943. Of all-welded, largely prefabricated construction, the hull was originally intended for merchant shipping, but was converted to combatant use by the U. S. Maritime Commission. The *Battler* displaced 11,420 tons, carried an air complement of eighteen planes, and featured a soda fountain and cafeteria, signs of her American birth. Her crew totalled seventy officers and four hundred fifty enlisted men. She was typical of a large number of escort carriers which helped to turn the tide in the Battle of the Atlantic.

Perhaps the most bizarre episode was a fight to the death between the blimp *K-34* and a U-boat. Airships were a valuable deterrent to submarine attack—none of the ships on the 89,000 voyages they escorted were lost—but no blimp had ever made an unassisted kill. Sighting a submarine lying on the surface off the coast of Florida, Lieutenant N. G. Grills launched an attack. Before the *K-34* could get into position to drop its depth charges, the Germans opened fire. With her gas envelope sliced open and helium draining away, the blimp settled upon the sea while the U-boat sailed away.

Between April 1943 and September 1944, when the Germans lost their submarine bases on the French coast, American and

British escort carriers sank thirty-three U-boats in the Atlantic and shared credit for the destruction of twelve others. An additional fourteen U-boats were sunk in Arctic waters as a result of their efforts. Carrier planes also damaged significant numbers of U-boats and directed surface ships in making kills in which they did not participate. But this is only part of the story. No one will ever know how many tons of shipping and supplies or how many lives had been saved by the apparently uneventful patrols of planes from the escort carriers that deterred U-boats from pressing home an attack.

The British were still haunted, though, by the threat of the *Tirpitz,* hiding in a Norwegian fjord. Even a false report on July 4, 1942 that she was at sea was enough for the Admiralty to order convoy PQ 17, bound for Murmansk, to scatter. With their covering cruisers and destroyers withdrawn, the luckless merchantmen

The *Huse,* an *Edsall*-class destroyer escort of 7,600 tons with an armament of three 3-inch guns, operates with an escort carrier on antisubmarine patrol in the Atlantic in December 1944. Mass-produced in enormous quantities, destroyer escorts provided adequate convoy escort, and helped turn the tide of the Battle of the Atlantic against the German U-boats.

Highline personnel transfer from the U.S. aircraft carrier *Wasp* to the destroyer *Overton* in the North Atlantic, late in 1941.

were picked off one by one by U-boats and German aircraft. Only thirteen of the thirty-six ships reached the safety of a Russian port. More than 3,000 vehicles, 430 tanks, 210 bombers and nearly 100,000 tons of general cargo were lost, and 153 merchant seamen died in the lifeboats and rafts that littered the frigid Arctic waters.

Following this disaster, the Admiralty suspended further convoys to Russia until they could be protected by aircraft carriers. Convoy PQ 18, which sailed from Iceland in September, included the escort carrier *Avenger*. As soon as the ships approached North Cape, they were attacked by six Junkers 88s which were beaten off by the *Avenger*'s dozen Hurricanes. Forty torpedo-carrying Heinkels 111s eluded the fighters, however, and sank eight merchantmen in eight minutes. Subsequent attacks over the next few days were broken up, with the fighters and the escort's antiaircraft fire accounting for forty-one bombers. U-boats also attacked the convoy, sinking three freighters while one of the submarines was sunk by the *Avenger*'s Swordfish.

But the *Tirpitz* remained a thorn in the side of the Royal Navy. Sizable Allied forces were tied down to keep watch for her, and every convoy bound for Russia had to have a powerful escort of capital ships in case the German battleship put to sea. U.S. Navy ships periodically joined the British fleet in these operations, among them the carriers *Wasp* and *Ranger*. Thirty SBDs and TBFs from the *Ranger* attacked German shipping in the Norwegian port of Bodø in October 1943, sinking five vessels and damaging seven others. Three American planes were lost, but the escorting Wildcats shot down two German aircraft.

Unable to bring the *Tirpitz* to action and sink her, the British tried to cripple her as she lay in Altenfjord, near North Cape. In September 1943, she was severely damaged by two miniature submarines called X-craft, which groped through a minefield and at-

A German U-boat being bombed and machine-gunned by a low-flying Allied aircraft. Caught on the surface, a German submarine had little chance, for her skin was thin and even slight damage could prevent her from submerging and, thus, escaping.

tached explosive charges to her hull. When the *Tirpitz* began coming to life again early in 1944, it was the turn of the Fleet Air Arm. Two strike forces, each consisting of twenty-one Barracuda bombers—a three-place monoplane designed to replace the Albacore and Swordfish—were embarked on the *Victorious* and *Furious*, while three escort carriers carried a large fighter screen. The waters of the fjord were too shallow for a torpedo attack, so ten of the planes carried 1,600-pound bombs which it was believed could penetrate the battleship's deck armor if dropped from more than 3,000 feet.

When the carriers had reached a point about 120 miles from the *Tirpitz's* lair at 0430 on April 30, 1944, the first wave of Barracudas took off into the dark. Flying at sea level to avoid the German radar, they climbed to 8,000 feet to cross the mountains. "It was the most beautiful morning," said Sub-Lieutenant Russell Jones. "A cloudless sky, the sea dead calm, and the snow on the mountains glowing pink in the morning sun. You could see for what seemed hundreds of miles."[39] The Germans were taken by surprise; first the fighters screamed down on the *Tirpitz* to suppress her antiaircraft batteries. The Barracudas followed up, diving to below 3,000 feet to make certain of hitting the target. Flames leaped from the vessel's hull and fountains of white water erupted about her. An

In general, German surface ships, such as these destroyers, could not operate in the North Sea or in the English Channel without close air support from the Luftwaffe.

A Barracuda returning from the attack on the *Tirpitz*.

Pride of the German Navy's surface fleet, the *Admiral von Tirpitz* was deployed to hide from Allied air attacks in Alta Fjord, off the small Norwegian island of Hakoya, in November 1944. Her eight 15-inch guns and 12¾-inch armor belt offered little protection from the "blockbuster" bombs used by British Lancaster bombers to sink her, shortly after this picture was taken by the ship's photographer.

hour later, another wave of bombers and fighters flew to the attack. In all, the *Tirpitz* was hit fourteen times, but the heavy bombs failed to pierce her armor because they had been dropped from too low an altitude. Even so, she was a shambles topside, her fire control system had been knocked out, she had been flooded, and 438 of her crew had been killed or wounded. The British lost two bombers.

Several other carrier-based attacks were launched on the *Tirpitz* as she was undergoing repairs during the summer of 1944. These scored no significant results. The battleship's seagoing career was over, however, for the continued presence of the escort carriers reduced the danger of an attack on the Russian convoys. The *Tirpitz* was towed to Tromso where she was to be used as floating battery to defend the Norwegian coast against an expected British invasion. R.A.F. Lancaster bombers found her there on November 12, 1944 and sank her with specially designed 6-ton "Tallboy" bombs.

9

"Get the Carriers!"

Two Japanese Bettys droned over the Pacific toward Bougainville on the morning of April 18, 1943. They were almost ready to land when sixteen U.S. Army P-38 Lightning fighters suddenly dropped out of the sun with guns blazing. While most of the Lightnings kept the escort of six Zeros occupied, a pair of the twin-tailed fighters concentrated on the bombers. Captain Thomas G. Lamphier came up behind one and riddled it with a long burst. Flames erupted from an engine, a wing broke off, and the plane smashed into the jungle below. The other Betty quickly followed it, crashing into the sea. Admiral Isoroku Yamamoto, Commander-in-Chief of the Combined Fleet, and most of his staff had been caught in a carefully prepared ambush.

Yamamoto's death came at a time of steady decline in the Imperial Navy's air strength. Following the capture of Guadalcanal, the Americans advanced up the Solomons archipelago, and edging around the southern tip of New Guinea, seized New Britain and Bougainville. Planes flying from Henderson Field and other land bases supported these operations so there was little need to call upon the U.S. Navy's carriers for support. It was just as well, for Admiral Halsey had only two ships, the *Saratoga* and the *Enterprise,* and the "Big E" was badly in need of a complete overhaul. With the pressure off in the Mediterranean, the British were persuaded to send the *Victorious* out to the Pacific to help fill the gap, but because of the extensive refit required before she could operate with an American fleet, she did not arrive in the combat zone until May 1943. Fortunately for the Allies, the Japanese did not take advantage of their superiority in carriers. Before his death, Yamamoto had ordered the carriers' planes ashore for massive

The TBF Avenger torpedo plane replaced the woefully inadequate Douglas Devastator following the Battle of Midway. The Avenger carried a 22-inch torpedo—or 2,000 pounds of bombs—at a speed of 267 mph. She enjoyed a maximum range of over 2,000 miles, and all later models carried some form of radar.

raids on Port Moresby and Guadalcanal, which were continued by his successor, Admiral Mineichi Koga. The results were negligible and many of the planes and their irreplaceable aircrews were lost.

Nine new fast carriers joined the fleet during the first six months of 1943, four of them of the 27,000-ton *Essex* class which could operate more than 100 aircraft. Speedy and well-armed, these vessels tipped the carrier balance in the Pacific toward the U.S. Navy. A new class of 11,000-ton light carriers, capable of handling thirty-five planes, was also joining the fleet. Large carrier task forces, defended by new battleships, including the 45,000-ton *New Jersey* class which bristled with antiaircraft guns, rode westward across the Pacific. In contrast to the situation during the grim days of 1942, when the Navy was reduced to one or two carriers, these new task forces consisted of a dozen flattops and a half-dozen

battleships. By the middle of 1943, the Navy had about 18,000 aircraft of all types. At the end of the following year, there were
30,000 planes.

There was also a corresponding increase in the quality of the
Navy's airplanes. The Wildcat was replaced by the Grumman F6F
Hellcat and the Chance-Vought F4U Corsair. The Hellcat was the
first shipborne fighter capable of defeating the latest model Zero.
Although less maneuverable than the Zero because of its weighty
armor and self-sealing tanks, the Hellcat had superior speed, altitude and performance. The huge gull-wing Corsair, which could
fly faster than 400 miles an hour, proved to be less satisfactory as
a carrier fighter because of its poor visibility and high landing
speed. But in the hands of shore-based Marine pilots it achieved
remarkable success. Major Gregory Boyington, one of the Marines'
top-scoring aces, won most of his 22 victories in a Corsair. (Boyington had earlier shot down six Japanese planes while serving

Commanding officer of Bombing Squadron 106, Commander John T. Hay-
ward (center) and other officers celebrating at an airbase in the South-
western Pacific, 1943–44.

During the closing phases of the campaign in the Solomon Islands in late 1943, the SBD Dauntless dive bombers took off from their Russell Islands air strip.

with the Flying Tigers in China.) Not all the new planes were considered improvements, however. Most pilots disliked the Curtiss SB2C Helldiver, even though it was faster, had a longer range, and carried a heavier bomb load than the much-admired SBD which it replaced as the Navy's first-line dive-bomber; the pilots called the unstable Helldiver "the Beast."

Halsey used his newfound strength to launch the first carrier raid on Rabaul on November 5, 1943. Task Force 38, built around the *Saratoga* and the light carrier *Princeton*, launched ninety-seven planes from the northern end of the Solomon Sea, about 230 miles southeast of the target. It was a "maximum effort" with no planes left behind to defend the carriers; that task was left to the land-based fighters from Henderson Field. Rain and overcast hid American carriers, but the sky was clear over Rabaul harbor, which was crammed with some fifty ships. In the ensuing attack, six cruisers and a destroyer were heavily damaged. As the bombers and torpedo planes made their runs, the escorting Hellcats tangled with seventy Japanese fighters which rose to meet them.

About twenty-five Japanese planes were shot down and an equal number listed as "probables," while the strike force lost ten planes. The Rabaul raid set the pattern for future carrier strikes against Japanese bases. Alarmed by the Americans' success, the Japanese flew in a hundred planes from their main base at Truk, thus further depleting their carrier air groups.

While amphibious forces under General Douglas MacArthur and Admiral Halsey worked their way through the southwest Pacific into a position to return to the Philippines, a new thrust across the central Pacific was launched. The newly organized Fifth Fleet was chosen to lead the way. Under the command of Vice Ad-

Once supreme in the Pacific, a Japanese B5N Kate torpedo bomber was blown to bits while attempting to attack an American carrier in the Marshall Islands in December 1943. The Kate's torpedo fell harmlessly into the calm seas.

miral Spruance, this armada initially included six large and six light carriers with about 700 aircraft, eight fast battleships and a sizable screen of cruisers and destroyers. The spearhead of the fleet was the Fast Carrier Task Force, designated as Task Force 58, and commanded by Rear Admiral Marc A. Mitscher, a grizzled pioneer naval aviator. TF58 was deployed in four task groups, each consisting of a mixture of large and light flattops and a screen. These groups operated individually or together as circumstances required. Improved communications and fighter detection techniques allowed them to maneuver and defend themselves to a degree not dreamed of in earlier carrier operations. The fleet was accompanied by a train of oilers, tenders and supply ships, ready to turn any remote atoll into a major base. The Fifth Fleet was thus the most powerful and most self-sufficient force yet seen in naval history.

The march across the central Pacific began on November 20, 1943 with the seizure of Tarawa in the Gilberts. Several hours of shelling and bombing were thought to have wiped out the Japanese, but they were cleverly hidden behind strong defenses and were ready when the Marines landed. Three days of desperate hand-to-hand fighting were required to root the Japanese out, and 1,000 Marines were killed while 2,000 were wounded. The entire 4,800-man Japanese garrison fought to the last rather than surrender.

Leapfrogging ahead, Spruance captured Kwajalein and Eniwetok in the Marshalls in January and February 1944. Having learned a bitter lesson at Tarawa, the Navy subjected these atolls to several days of bombing and bombardment. Consequently, about half the defenders had been killed before the Marines and Army troops were landed.

Meanwhile, Admiral Mitscher's carriers struck at Truk, the "Gibraltar of the Pacific." Anticipating an attack, Admiral Koga, Commander-in-Chief of the Combined Fleet, had ordered most of his warships to Palau, but a large number of merchantmen were left behind. Early on the morning of February 17, 1944, seventy Hellcats attacked the island's airfields, shooting down more than thirty of the planes "scrambled" to meet them and destroying another forty on the ground. Eighteen TBFs followed with fragmentation bombs and incendiaries while dive bombers sank thirty

A PB4Y-1 patrol bomber of VB 106 crash-lands on Munda airfield in February 1944.

The crew of "Mitzi-Bishi," a PB4Y-1 Liberator patrol bomber of Bombing Squadron 106, poses with its aircraft during Pacific operations in 1943–44.

The escort carrier *Manila Bay*, ferrying USAAF P-47 fighters to the Marianas under bombing attack by four Japanese Zeke fighters off Saipan in June 1944.

merchant ships, including a 19,000-ton tanker, in round-the-clock raids. A couple of cruisers and destroyers were also sunk and 275 planes were shot down. For the first time, the U.S. Navy used special radar-equipped TBFs to conduct night bombing operations which accounted for a significant segment of the ships sunk. Truk was finished as an important Japanese base. The Combined Fleet now retreated to Tawi Tawi off northeastern Borneo, to be closer to its fuel supplies.

Having knocked out Truk, Admiral Nimitz decided, rather than occupying the island, to bypass it and make a 1,000-mile leap across the Pacific to Guam, Saipan and Tinian in the Marianas. These islands were to be used as springboards for attacks on the Japanese homeland, only 1,500 miles away, by long-range bombers and submarines. Unlike previous American conquests, these islands were within the Japanese defense perimeter and their loss would disrupt vital lines of communication with the conquered territory to the south. Admiral Soemu Toyoda, who had become the Imperial Navy's senior officer after Admiral Koga disappeared on a flight to the Philippines, decided to give battle at the first opportunity.

Since the last major air-sea action off Santa Cruz, the Japanese had rebuilt their carrier strength to nine ships, including the

160

33,000-ton *Taiho*, which had an armored flight deck like the British flattops. New planes had also been developed, including an improved Zero fighter, the Jill torpedo plane, and the Judy dive bomber, which was almost as fast as the Hellcat. But the Japanese lacked experienced pilots and aircrews, so that men were sent to the carriers with little training. "The Navy was frantic for pilots," said one Japanese flying instructor. "Men who could never have dreamed even of getting near a fighter plane before the war were now thrown into the battle."

Upon receiving reports of the American landing at Saipan on June 15, 1944, the Japanese fleet, under command of Admiral Jis-

An F6F Hellcat successfully lands aboard the *Yorktown* despite the loss of her tailhook. Named after the sunken veteran of the Battle of Midway, the new *Yorktown* was one of twenty-four *Essex*-class carriers. Displacing 27,100 tons, capable of making 33 knots, and carrying up to 110 aircraft, the *Essex* class formed the backbone of the victorious American task forces during the last two years of the Pacific war.

Carrier crewmen exult as an attacking Japanese plane hits the water during a raid by Task Force 58 on the Marianas in late February 1944.

aburo Ozawa, sailed from its base at Tawi Tawi in three groups. The van included the light carriers *Zuiho, Chitose* and *Chiyoda,* supported by four battleships: the *Yamato* and *Musashi* with their 18-inch guns, and the old *Haruna* and *Kongo*; Force A included Ozawa's flagship the *Taiho,* and the *Shokaku* and *Zuikaku*; and Force B included the *Hiyo, Junyo,* the smaller *Ryuho,* and another battleship. In all, the Japanese had about 475 aircraft. Ranged against them were the fifteen carriers and seven battleships of TF58 under Marc Mitscher, who flew his flag in the new carrier *Lexington.* Although the Americans had 956 planes, double the Japanese strength, Ozawa had certain advantages. He expected to fight within range of Japanese aircraft on Guam and the adjacent islands, and his planes had greater range than those of the Americans. This meant that he could strike the American carriers while remaining beyond their reach. And unlike Admiral Spruance, the overall American commander, his hands were not tied by the need to protect the beachhead on Saipan.

As soon as his submarines informed him of the approach of the Japanese fleet, Spruance postponed a landing on Guam that had been scheduled for June 18. TF58's carrier groups were positioned to the west of Saipan on a line perpendicular to the wind so they could turn in and out of it to launch and receive planes without interfering with each other. Seven battleships flying the flag of Vice Admiral Willis A. Lee took up a position between the carriers and the approaching Japanese. On June 17, Spruance gave Mitscher his battle plan, which was simplicity itself:

Our air will first knock out enemy carriers, then will attack enemy battleships and cruisers to slow or disable them. Battle Line will de-

On the morning of May 21, 1943, an F4F Wildcat missed the arrestor cable while trying to land on the large American carrier *Lexington*. The pilot attempted to veer off the deck but his engine stalled and his tail hook caught on a protrusion, snapping the aircraft against the port side catwalk. Before the plane was worked free—to dive "nose down" into the water—lines were lowered to save the pilot.

stroy enemy fleet either by fleet action if the enemy elects to fight or by sinking slowed or crippled ships if enemy retreats. Action against the enemy must be pushed vigorously by all hands to ensure complete destruction of his fleet.

Late on June 18, the Japanese fleet was sighted about 350 miles to the west in the Philippine Sea. The aggressive Mitscher wanted to close the enemy during the night so he would be able to launch his planes at dawn at little more than 200 miles from the Japanese carriers, but Spruance refused permission. He was concerned that Ozawa had divided his fleet into several units, which might leave one of them free to destroy the Saipan beachhead while Mitscher was diverted by another. "End run by other carrier groups remain possibility," he told Mitscher, but this explanation did little to lessen the disappointment of Mitscher and his flyers who felt they were being denied the opportunity to strike the first blow.

The Battle of the Philippine Sea began soon after dawn on June 19. The day was fair and clear, but from the direction of Guam there appeared a tiny thunderhead in the form of a few Japanese aircraft. Hellcats darted after them and one soon reported: "Tally-hoed two Judys; splash one." More Japanese planes were re-

In Simpson Harbor, Rabaul, a Japanese heavy cruiser of the *Nachi* class attempted to escape from attacks by American aircraft from the carriers *Princeton* and *Saratoga* on November 2, 1943.

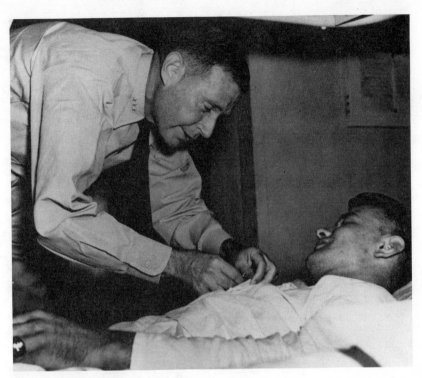

Vice Admiral Raymond A. Spruance.

ported to be taking off from Orote Field on Guam so Mitscher sent in thirty-three Hellcats to deal with them. About thirty enemy fighters and bombers were shot down or destroyed on the ground. Shortly before 1000 the Hellcats received the signal from the *Lexington* to return—"Hey Rube!"—the old circus call for help. The first wave of Japanese carrier planes had been picked up on radar while they were still 140 miles to the west.

Ozawa had launched his first strike of 69 planes at 0830; about a half-hour later a second wave of 128 planes followed. Just after taking off, Warrant Officer Sakio Komatsu sighted a torpedo that had been fired by the American submarine *Albacore* streaking for the *Taiho*. He nosed his plane over into a suicide dive and exploded the torpedo before it struck. But another torpedo smashed into the carrier's starboard side. The damage appeared moderate— a jammed forward elevator and some fuel lines weakened—and the *Taiho* continued combat operations.

165

The F6F Hellcat began to replace the Wildcat as America's standard naval fighter in late 1943. With a speed of 376 mph and an armament of either six 50-cal. machine guns or four 20-mm cannon, the Hellcat could out-fly and out-gun the Japanese Zero. The Hellcat's rugged construction enabled it to withstand damage that the lightly armored Japanese fighter could not.

Mitscher ordered every available Hellcat into the air to meet the incoming Japanese. The carriers' flight decks exploded into what has been described as "carefully controlled frenzy." Plane handlers in blue shirts and helmets, plane directors in yellow, hookmen in green, chockmen in purple, and firefighters in red scurried about, readying the planes for launching. Pilots hoisted themselves into their cockpits and, with a howl and rush, the big Hellcats hurtled into the sky, to be vectored out to their targets by the fighter directors in the Combat Information Centers. To provide room for the fighters to land, refuel and rearm, Mitscher ordered all torpedo and dive bombers into the air. Unable to reach the Japanese carriers which were some 400 miles away, they were to orbit on the eastern—or unengaged—side of the task force. Within minutes, 140 Hellcats had been put into the air to join the eighty that were already airborne and, as they flew to meet the Japanese, climbed to over 25,000 feet.

The two forces collided about ninety miles from the American carriers. Pushing the charging handles of their six .50-caliber guns and checking their gunsights, the Hellcat pilots nosed down on the sixty-nine Japanese planes spread out below them. Commander Charles W. Brewer, leader of Fighting Squadron 15 (VF 15) from the *Essex*, reported that his initial burst of gunfire literally ripped a Zero to pieces. Before the debris had hit the sea, Brewer was already on the tail of another enemy fighter. He accounted for two more Zeros during the brief battle.

Japanese planes were "falling like leaves," said one pilot, and those that escaped got only as far as the line of battleships pro-

On the night of April 29–30, 1944, an OS2U Kingfisher catapult-launched scout plane rescued nine Navy fliers downed during an air strike against the key Japanese base at Truk in the Carolines. Skimming along the water, the Kingfisher made contact with the American submarine *Tang*, which took the rescued crewmen aboard. The slow, low-powered Kingfisher was famed during the war for many such rescues in combat areas.

A TDR-1 assault drone being prepared for an attack on the Japanese strong-hold of Rabaul, probably late in 1943.

tecting the carriers before they were shot down by antiaircraft guns firing shells fitted with the new VT, or proximity fuse, which automatically detonated them within seventy feet of a target. The only hit was on the *South Dakota*, which lost twenty-seven men but suffered no reduction in her fighting capacity. In all, forty-two Japanese planes were shot down by the Hellcats and the screen. No enemy aircraft reached the carriers and only one American fighter was lost.

A half-hour later, Hellcats tore into the second and largest wave of Japanese planes. Once again, VF 15, led by Commander David McCampbell, skipper of the *Essex*'s air group, was the first into action. He dived into a formation of Judy dive bombers again

168

and again, shooting down four and claiming a probable before running out of ammunition. Later in the day, McCampbell accounted for three more Japanese planes. By the time the war ended, he was the Navy's leading ace with thirty-four victories and the Medal of Honor.

Other squadrons joined in the melee and the radio circuits crackled with a riotous mixture of shouts, curses, warnings and cries of encouragement. "Hell, this is like an old time turkey shoot!" yelled one pilot—and thus the battle became known as the "Great Marianas Turkey Shoot." About twenty enemy planes broke through the Hellcats but most were disposed of by the battleships' guns. Six Judys reached the *Wasp* and *Bunker Hill* but did little damage. Of the 109 planes which had attacked TF 58, only about fifteen survived.

Lieutenant (jg) Alexander Vraciu of VF 16 had one of the strangest experiences of the day. Shortly after taking off from the *Lexington*, the engine of his Hellcat began to leak oil and he was ordered to orbit the carrier along with five other cripples. Vraciu, who already had thirteen victories to his credit, spotted a flock of Judys heading for the *Lexington*. With a couple of wingmates he

SBD dive bombers from the *Lexington* flew over the invasion site on Saipan on D-Day, June 15, 1944.

dived in among them, pushing his plane to within 200 feet of a Judy's tail before opening fire. The Japanese plane exploded into fragments and Vraciu shouted: "Scratch one Judy!" Two more enemy planes fell before his guns and the Japanese "began to separate like a bunch of disorderly cattle," he recalled. "Every time one of the Japs would try to lead a string of others out of the formation, the Hellcat pilots turned into 'cowboys' and herded them back into the group. If they had been able to scatter, we wouldn't have shot down as many as we did."[40] Vraciu ran his total to six and was chasing another Judy when it was shot down by antiaircraft fire. Suddenly, the sky was empty of enemy planes and the Hellcats headed for their carriers. Later, Vraciu learned that he had expended only 360 rounds of ammunition in winning his half-dozen victories.

Trails of American and Japanese fighters marked the sky during the Marianas "Turkey Shoot." Although the number of trained Japanese pilots actually increased after the Battle of Midway, during the campaign for the Solomons the Japanese lost the best of their educated aviators whom their pilot training failed to replace.

Admiral King believed that the key to the Pacific campaign was the seizure of the Mariana Islands. Here, six American TBF bombers are enroute to strike Pagan Island on June 23, 1944.

Mitscher did not neglect Orote Field on Guam. At about 1300, the Helldivers and Avengers that had been slowly orbiting to the east of the carriers were ordered to bomb the strip and to make it unusable for straggling survivors of the air battles. Japanese anti-aircraft fire was heavy but the attackers cratered the runway with 500- and 1,000-pound bombs, and destroyed several planes on the ground.

Admiral Ozawa, not realizing the magnitude of the Japanese losses, continued to feed planes into the battle. A third strike consisting of forty-nine planes was flown off but half failed to find the American fleet, and so returned to their carriers. The others were ambushed by Hellcats and seven were shot down, while the rest attacked one of the American carrier groups with little effect. A fourth wave of eighty-two planes followed. Those that were not accounted for by the combat air patrols or the fierce antiaircraft fire were bagged trying to land on Guam. Only nine survived.

Ozawa was also being harassed by American submarines. Short-ly before noon, the *Cavalla* got in among the Japanese ships and fired a spread of three torpedoes into the *Shokaku*. The carrier caught fire and blew up about three hours later, and few of her 1,263 officers and men were picked up. Not long afterward, a similar fate befell the *Taiho*. Fumes from the fuel lines that had been weakened by the torpedo explosion that morning were ignited and her armored flight deck was ripped away by the blast. Ozawa transferred his flag to a destroyer but only about 500 of the *Taiho's* crew of 2,150 were rescued before she capsized and sank.

The sky over TF58 had been swept clear of enemy aircraft by late afternoon. Two Japanese carriers had been sunk by submarines and a phenomenal 373 planes had been shot down. Mitscher had lost only twenty-three aircraft through enemy action and not one of his ships had been seriously damaged. The U.S. Navy had emerged victorious from the greatest carrier battle of the war.

Free at last of his concern that the Japanese might outflank TF58 and attack the beachhead at Saipan, Admiral Spruance gave Mitscher permission to go after the seven remaining Japanese carriers. Ozawa had only about 100 planes left, but because of highly colored reports, the Admiral believed that the Americans had suffered even worse than he, and that many of his missing aircraft had landed on Guam. He therefore planned to again offer battle on the next day, after refueling. American reconnaissance aircraft sighted the enemy fleet late on July 20, as it lay just within range. Mitscher now faced a dilemma. If he launched his planes, they would return in the dark with nearly empty tanks, and few of his pilots were experienced in night landings. But if he waited until daylight, he might lose his last opportunity to destroy the Japanese fleet. "Launch 'em," declared the taciturn Mitscher. In six-inch-high letters, his orders were chalked on all the ready-room blackboards: "Get the Carriers!"

Within ten minutes, 216 aircraft—seventy-seven dive bombers, fifty-three torpedo planes and eighty-six fighters—lifted off the flight decks of ten carriers and headed into the setting sun. Flying carefully to conserve fuel, they found part of the Japanese fleet just before sundown. Ozawa managed to put about seventy-five planes into the air but they were not enough to halt the strike. A pair of oilers, which were trailing the fleet, were so badly damaged that they were abandoned by their crews. Then the American planes caught up with the carrier *Hiyo*.

A TBF with a damaged wingtip landed on the Hornet during the Marianas operation on June 13, 1944.

Several Avengers, including one piloted by Lieutenant (jg) George B. Brown, began runs on the vessel in the face of heavy flak. Brown was badly wounded, his plane caught fire and part of a wing was shot away. The radioman and gunner bailed out, but when the fire burned itself out, Brown pressed home the attack. His torpedo apparently struck the *Hiyo*, and a wingmate tried to lead his plane, which was steering erratically, back toward TF58. Brown disappeared into a cloud, however, and was never seen again. In the meantime, the *Hiyo*, which had been hit by another torpedo, caught fire and sank. The *Zuikaku*, *Junyo* and *Chiyoda* were damaged, and the Japanese lost another sixty-five aircraft. As he withdrew in the direction of Okinawa, Admiral Ozawa had

173

During the Battle of the Philippine Sea on the night of June 20, 1944, hundreds of American aircraft found their way back to their carriers of Task Force 58 when Vice Admiral Marc Mitscher decided, against all wartime practice, to turn on the running lights.

only three-dozen or so planes left, out of the more than 400 that had crowded the flight decks of his carriers the previous morning.

Bombs and torpedoes expended, the Americans started the flight back to their carriers in ones and twos. As Mitscher had foreseen, night had closed in by the time they returned and only a few of the more skilled pilots—or the luckier ones—managed to land on the darkened flight decks. Most of the returning pilots could make out the ships' wakes but could not distinguish the carriers from the other large ships. On the carriers, planes were heard circling overhead, some flashing red and green recognition lights, engines coughing and sputtering as they ran out of fuel. There were heavy splashes as some "ditched" in the black sea. Every eye was on "Pete" Mitscher as he sat slumped in a chair in the flag plot of the *Lexington*, torn between identification with his pilots and the danger that the fleet might attract enemy submarines if it were lit up. Decision made, he turned to Captain Arleigh Burke, his chief of staff, and ordered, "Turn on the lights."

174

Carriers switched on their red masthead lights, glow lights outlined the flight decks, searchlights lit up the sky and some ships fired star shells. The Philippine Sea was transformed into a Mardi Gras. One pilot said it was like "a Hollywood premiere, Chinese New Year's and the Fourth of July rolled into one." Planes landed on any flattop they could find and some crashed into aircraft that had already been landed. One even mistook the truck light of a destroyer for the signal of a landing control officer and made a perfect landing in the sea beside her. By 2200 every plane had either landed or "ditched" and the carriers steamed away. Destroyers and float planes remained behind to search for downed airmen, and although about a hundred planes were lost, almost ninety percent of the flyers were saved.

10

To the Heart of Japan

Coughing and sputtering, the engines of the Wildcats and Avengers flown by Escort Carrier Group Three—"Taffy 3"— roared into life at sunup on October 25, 1944. Lifting off from the half-dozen "jeep" carriers that lay off Samar in the central Philippines, they headed for nearby Leyte to support the Army troops landed five days before by General MacArthur. Operations were proceeding routinely when an urgent warning was received from a patrol plane: Four enemy battleships, and a flock of cruisers and destroyers were approaching at high speed from the north. "Air plot, tell him to check his identification," replied an irritated Rear Admiral Clifton A. F. Sprague, certain that the pilot had misidentified some American ships. "Identification of enemy force confirmed," the pilot answered. "Ships have pagoda masts!"[41]

Sprague's unsuspecting vessels had been catapulted by a series of mishaps into the center of the greatest sea battle in history— the Battle for Leyte Gulf.

Following the Battle of the Philippine Sea and the loss of Saipan and Guam, Japan had been so weakened that a bold leap across 1,500 miles of sea to Leyte was feasible. The target date for the landing was originally mid-December, but it was moved up when Admiral Halsey, Spruance's successor as commander of the Fifth Fleet, now designated the Third Fleet, raided the Philippines and discovered that Japanese resistance was surprisingly weak. In two days, 173 enemy planes were shot down, another 305 were destroyed on the ground and fifty-nine ships of various types sunk.

To prevent Japan's remaining air strength from interfering with the impending invasion, the Fast Carrier Task Force—now designated TF38 but still under Mitscher's command—struck at For-

Crewmen of the *Hancock* moving rockets to planes for use in the raid on Formosa of October 12, 1944. The successful attack was designed to draw out and destroy Japanese aircraft which might have been used to oppose the Leyte landings which occurred a few days later.

mosa on October 12. Admiral Shigeru Fukudome, who had put all his 230 fighters into the air to oppose the strike, reported:

A terrific aerial combat began directly above my head. Our interceptors swooped down in great force at the invading enemy planes. Our planes appeared to do so well that I thought I could desire no better performance. In a matter of moments, one after the other, planes were seen falling down, enveloped in flames. 'Well done! Well done! A tremendous success!' I clapped my hands. Alas! To my sudden disappointment, a closer watch revealed that all those shot down were *our* fighters, and all those proudly circling above our heads were enemy planes! Our fighters were nothing but so many eggs thrown at the stone wall of the indomitable enemy formation. In a brief one-sided encounter, the combat terminated in our total defeat.[42]

Forty-eight American planes were lost to the intensive Japanese antiaircraft fire but they destroyed more than a third of the enemy's air strength. An additional forty Betty bombers launching torpedo attacks against the task force were also shot down. Over the next two days, the Japanese attacked the fleet with all the planes that had been accumulated to replace the carrier air groups lost in the Philippine Sea. More than 600 aircraft were lost. These losses exceeded those of the Luftwaffe during the entire Battle of Britain. Only two American cruisers were damaged and seventy-nine planes lost. The Japanese claimed to have sunk almost the entire fleet, which prompted Halsey to sardonically report he was "retiring toward the enemy following the salvage of

On October 20, 1944, high over Leyte Gulf, a FM-2 Wildcat flew combat air cover over the escort carrier *Santee* as the American invasion forces stabbed into the heart of the Japanese-occupied Philippines. Although replaced on the fleet carriers by the F6F Hellcat in 1943, the Wildcat continued to serve throughout the war on the smaller escort carriers. Valiant attacks by bombless Wildcats during the Battle off Samar confused the inept Japanese commander and he broke off the engagement, despite the fact that he was about to achieve tactical victory and could have destroyed the Leyte invasion transports.

the Third Fleet ships recently reported sunk by Radio Tokyo."

Following this foray, the carriers of TF38 provided support for MacArthur's invasion of Leyte. Only thirty Zeros and an equal number of Betty bombers and a few Army planes were able to survive the triphammer American attacks upon the Japanese airfields. The landing thus proceeded without serious air interference. Immediately upon receiving word of the invasion, however, the Japanese put their long prepared Shō-1, or Victory, Plan into operation. This plan, a daring and desperate mixture of stealth and ruse, depended upon surprise and Japanese superiority in night operations for success.

Two fleets were to converge like a giant pincers on Leyte Gulf where they were to sink the transports and supply ships of Ad-

A comrade tightened the ancient Hachimaki scarf around the head of every kamikaze pilot before he took off on his suicide mission. Worn by the revered Samurai warriors, the cloth had both symbolic and practical benefits: it represented manly courage and composure before battle, and it confined long hair, while keeping perspiration out of the eyes.

The U.S. Navy's leading fighter ace, Commander David McCampbell, wing commander of the *Essex*, shown here in October 1944 with thirty "kills." Flying an F6F Hellcat, McCampbell downed more enemy planes in a single sortie—nine—than any other American fighter pilot.

181

THIS BOOK PROPERTY OF
STANLEY J. BLAZEWSKI
519 W 2ND AV ROSSELLE NJ

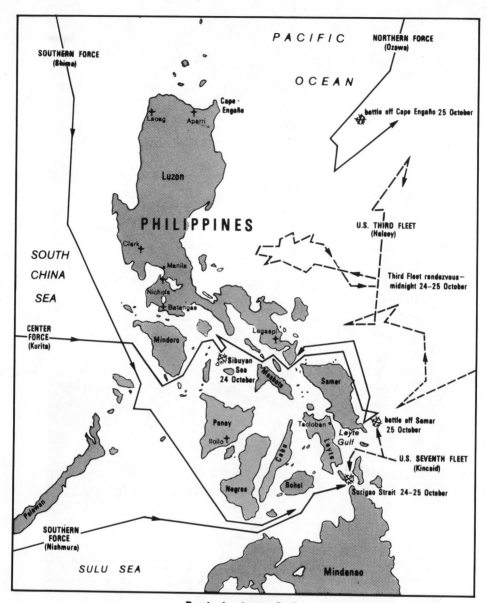

Battle for Leyte Gulf
24–26 October 1944

- - - - - U.S. Naval forces
———— Japanese Naval forces
+ Major Japanese airfield

0 ———————— 100
Miles

miral Thomas C. Kinkaid's Seventh Fleet, and cut off the American beachhead. The stronger of the Japanese forces, under the command of Vice Admiral Takeo Kurita, consisted of five battleships, including the giant *Yamato* and *Musashi*. It was to pass through the San Bernardino Strait to the north of Leyte. The other force, which included two old battleships under the command of Vice Admiral Shoji Nishimura, was to transit the Surigao Strait to the south. Although Admiral Ozawa's four remaining carriers could muster only 116 planes among them, they were the key to the operation. They were to come south from the Japanese home islands toward Luzon and were to lure Halsey and his ships away from Leyte. To make up for the shortage of experienced pilots, the Japanese had also devised a new and terrifying weapon—the Divine Wind, or Kamikaze Corps—whose members had sworn to dive their bomb-laden aircraft into enemy ships.

U.S. Navy submarines and aircraft had taken such a heavy toll of the Imperial Navy's fuel stocks that the ships involved in Shō-1 took nearly a week to arrive off Leyte. This delay cost them any chance to surprise the Americans, and meant sacrificing the opportunity to attack Kinkaid's vessels while they were still unloading. First blood was drawn on October 23 by two American submarines, the *Darter* and *Dace*, which sank two of Kurita's cruisers, including his flagship the *Atago*, in the South China Sea.

The Japanese struck back the next day. The planes that had been flown to the Philippines were grouped in three waves of fifty to sixty planes each. These attacked one of Halsey's carrier groups. The first wave was met by seven Hellcats from the *Essex*, led by Commander David McCampbell. Within a half-hour, McCampbell and his wingman, Lieutenant Roy W. Rushing, shot down fifteen enemy planes—nine by McCampbell, who set a record for one mission in the Pacific war. "After following the decimated formation nearly all the way to Manila, we returned . . . nearly exhausted of ammunition and near fuel-exhaustion," he said.[43] Upon landing, McCampbell found he had "barely sufficient gas to taxi out of the arresting gear."

Another group of Japanese aircraft attacked the light carrier *Princeton*. "We held off eighty planes for fifteen minutes . . . shooting down twenty-eight," reported Lieutenant Carl Brown, one of the ship's fighter pilots. "Ordinarily, we would not have tackled eighty planes with eight Hellcats, but it was get them before they got our ships. . . . We went after them with all guns and throttles wide open."[44]

Nevertheless, they could not save the carrier. A lone Judy slipped undetected out of the clouds and dropped two 500-pound bombs on the *Princeton*; these smashed into her hangar deck, starting fierce fires. Six torpedo-armed Avengers exploded, adding to the flames. All men not needed to fight the flames were ordered to abandon ship and were taken off by the cruiser *Birmingham* and several destroyers. Tons of water were poured into the stricken carrier while Hellcats drove off enemy planes trying to attack her. By mid-afternoon, all the fires had been extinguished except for a blaze near the stern that was approaching the torpedo storage area.

Pilots of Torpedo Squadron 13 in the ready room of the *Franklin* before taking part in the Battle of Sibuyan Sea, in which the incredible number of eighteen to twenty torpedo hits were required to sink the Japanese super-battleship *Musashi*.

The 64,170-ton Japanese battleship *Yamato* under attack by American Hell-diver dive bombers in the Battle of the Sibuyan Sea in October 1944. The *Yamato* was the largest and most heavily armed battleship ever constructed, and surely one of the most durable. Despite negligible combat air protection by Japanese aircraft, and a sustained and intensive assault by an American carrier task force, only two hits bombs struck the *Yamato,* both on or near the "A" turret, which suffered rather slight damage. Indeed, her sister ship, the *Musashi,* succumbed in the same action only after suffering twenty hits by torpedoes dropped by hostile aircraft and perhaps more launched by an American submarine.

The *Birmingham* had come alongside again to help prepare the *Princeton* for towing when a violent blast blew off her stern, raining huge pieces of flaming debris down on the cruiser.

"The spectacle which greeted the human eye was horrible to behold," said one of the cruiser's officers. "Dead, dying and wounded, many of them badly and horribly, covered the decks . . . Blood ran freely down our waterways, and continued to run for some time."[45] The *Birmingham* was only slightly damaged but 229 of her men had been killed and 420 wounded. The *Princeton* was now beyond salvage and she was abandoned and torpedoed—the first American flattop to be lost since the old *Hornet* had been sunk in the Solomons two years before.

TF38 soon exacted its revenge. Aabout 250 carrier planes attacked Kurita's fleet in the Sibuyan Sea to the northwest of Leyte.

185

The Japanese had little in the way of air cover, but with the *Yamato* and *Musashi* each mounting 120 guns their antiaircraft fire was intense. The *Musashi* bore the full brunt of the attack. She was attacked again and again, but eight torpedo and four bomb hits merely slowed down the well-protected vessel. It took another ten torpedoes and a half-dozen more direct bomb hits before she finally capsized and sank, taking nearly half of her 2,400 officers and men with her. Several of Kurita's other battleships, including the *Yamato,* were damaged, but the airmen overestimated the effectiveness of their attacks and the Japanese continued to press on towards the San Bernardino Strait and Kinkaid's transports.

In the meantime, Kinkaid had been warned of the approach of Admiral Nishimura's southern force. Correctly surmising that the Japanese were heading for the Surigao Strait, he placed his six old battleships—the *West Virginia, Tennessee, California, Maryland, Pennsylvania* and *Mississippi*—across the northern end of the strait, to intercept the enemy ships. Entering those waters in the early-morning hours of October 25, Nishimura was first harassed by destroyers and PT boats, and then found his way blocked by the American battleships, which were under the command of Rear Admiral Jesse B. Oldendorf. They poured 14- and 16-inch shells down upon Nishimura's ships, and two Japanese battleships were sunk. The U.S. Navy had won the last naval battle ever fought in a formal line, a triumph made sweeter by the fact that most of the victorious fleet were ships that had been raised from the mud of Pearl Harbor.

Earlier that evening, Admiral Halsey had learned of the approach of Ozawa's four carriers from the north, and not knowing that they were "paper tigers" almost empty of aircraft, itched to attack them. He eagerly accepted the overly optimistic claims made by his pilots about the damage they had inflicted upon Kurita's force. Convincing himself that Kinkaid was strong enough to deal with Kurita, Halsey regarded the approaching flattops as his most important target—just as the Japanese intended. "I went into flag plot," he wrote in his memoirs, "put my finger on the Northern Force's charted position, 300 miles away, and said, 'Here's where we're going . . . start them north.' "[46]

Halsey's action left the San Bernardino Strait wide open—and

Kurita steamed through it undetected that night. Kinkaid had been informed of Halsey's decision to pursue Ozawa, but having intercepted a confusing directive from the admiral, believed that newly organized Task Force 34 was being left to watch the passage. Halsey, for his part, was convinced that Kinkaid was maintaining surveillance of the area. Thus, each commander supposed that the other was guarding the San Bernardino Strait, and neither was. Despite heavy Japanese losses, the Shō Plan seemed to be working, for nothing now stood in the way of Kurita's battleships and the American invasion fleet—except for Kinkaid's fragile escort carriers.

Eighteen of the vessels were deployed in three groups of six, each with a screen of seven destroyers and destroyer escorts a short distance seaward of Leyte Gulf. The southernmost, "Taffy 1" was commanded by Rear Admiral Thomas Sprague in the *Sangamon*; then came "Taffy 2" under Rear Admiral Felix Stump in the *Natoma Bay*, while "Taffy 3" under Clifton Sprague in the *Fanshaw Bay*, was off Samar and closest to the advancing Japanese. His other ships were the *St. Lo*, *White Plains*, *Kalinin Bay*, *Kitkun Bay* and *Gambier Bay*.

Kurita opened fire on the escort carriers as soon as they were sighted and his shells, filled with varied-colored dyes, exploded about them, raising geysers of purple and yellow sea water. "Hey, they're shooting at us in technicolor!," cried one American seaman.[47] This was the first time—and the last—that the *Yamato*'s massive guns were fired at an enemy ship. As startled by the unexpected appearance of Sprague's vessels as Sprague was to see the Japanese, Kurita mistook "Taffy 3" for Halsey's fast carriers and battleships. Instead of leaving a few cruisers behind to quickly dispose of the "jeeps" and plunging ahead with his fleet to wreak havoc on Kinkaid's helpless transports and cargo vessels, he diverted his entire force to an attack on "Taffy 3."

"I didn't think we'd last fifteen minutes," Sprague said later, but "I thought we might as well give them all we've got before we go down." There was no precedent in naval history for the action that followed, in which a handful of puny escort carriers took on a fleet of battleships and cruisers. Sprague hurriedly laid down a smokescreen and launched the remainder of his Avengers and Wildcats, arming them with any weapons available—heavy bombs,

187

fragmentation bombs, torpedoes, even depth charges. As soon as the planes were aloft his six ships dodged in and out of a rain squall that providentially concealed them from the enemy guns. When his motley collection of planes ran out of bombs and torpedoes, they strafed the Japanese ships with machine-gun fire. Then, ammunition expended, they made passes at the ships in hope of distracting the enemy gunners. These dummy runs forced the Japanese ships to make frequent changes in course so they were unable to make use of their superior speed to close the range with the carriers which were fleeing south. One pilot, Lieutenant Paul B. Garrison, made twenty strafing runs, ten of them with empty guns.

"Taffy 2" and "Taffy 3" answered Sprague's pleas for help and sent their planes to his assistance. Kinkaid also ordered Oldendorf's half-dozen battleships north at flank speed, but they were more than 130 miles away from the battle. "The enemy was closing with disconcerting rapidity and the volume of fire was increasing,"

During the Battle of Leyte Gulf, the escort carrier *Gambier Bay* and two destroyer escorts make smoke and desperately try to escape the surprise appearance of Admiral Kurita's battleship-cruiser force off Samar, October 25. The unlucky *Gambier Bay*, two destroyers and a destroyer escort were sunk by the Japanese in this action.

Admiral King claimed that the Japanese would fight to the last man, and his prediction was bolstered by Japanese behavior throughout the Pacific War. As the *Zuikaku* listed to port after being hit aft by an American torpedo bomber, her crew stood at attention on her deck to salute the Rising Sun one last time as the flag was lowered from her mast. The *Zuikaku*, the finest product of Japanese technology, was inferior to equivalent American aircraft carriers, a fact which symbolized the backwardness of Japan's primitive economic structure. However, the *Zuikaku* had a long career, launching planes against Pearl Harbor in 1941, and helping to sink the American carriers *Lexington* and *Hornet* the following year.

Sprague reported. "At this point it did not appear that any of our ships could survive another five minutes of the heavy-caliber fire being received." Faced with "the ultimate in desperate circumstances," he ordered his destroyer screen to launch a torpedo attack. "Small boys . . . intercept!" he radioed.[48]

"We need a bugler to sound the charge," declared Commander Amos T. Hathaway as his ship, the *Heerman*, and the *Hoel* and *Johnson* dashed to within point-blank range of the enemy before firing their torpedoes. Six tin fish from the *Heerman* forced the *Yamato* to veer temporarily out of the fight and one from the *John-*

son struck the cruiser *Kumano*, disabling her. Having expended their torpedoes, the destroyers peppered the heavily armored Japanese ships with 5-inch shells. But the enemy's big guns soon found their target and the *Johnson* was hit by a salvo of shells, and sunk. "It was like a puppy being smacked by a truck," said one of her surviving officers.

The escort carriers had emerged from the protection of the rain squall and several of them were hit, the most seriously the *Gambier Bay*. Ablaze and losing speed, she dropped behind her consorts. The remaining destroyers tried to help her, but she was too far gone and capsized. The *Kalinin Bay* was hit sixteen times and Sprague reported:

The shells created a shambles below decks, her officers told me later, and only the heroic efforts of her crew kept the little ship going. Bos'n's crews wrestled under five feet of water to plug up big holes in the hull; engineers worked knee-deep in oil, choking in the stench of burned rubber; quartermasters steered the ship for hours from an emergency wheel below, as fire scorched the deck on which they stood, and all hands risked their lives to save mates in flooded or burning compartments.[49]

Where was Halsey and the bulk of the Third Fleet? At about the same time the Japanese gunners were opening up on the escort carriers, TF38 launched the first of six attacks against Admiral Ozawa's carriers which had been found about 200 miles east of Cape Engaño at the northeastern tip of Luzon. The handful of planes carried by the four Japanese carriers were quickly brushed aside but the fleet's antiaircraft fire was intense. The *Chitose* was bombed and sunk, and the flagship *Zuikaku* was so badly damaged by a torpedo that Ozawa transferred his flag to a cruiser. The *Zuiho* was also damaged during this strike. The second wave of American planes disabled the *Chiyoda*, the only undamaged Japanese flattop.

The *Zuikaku* was hit by three more torpedoes during the third strike, and the last survivor of the Pearl Harbor raiding force rolled over and sank. The fourth strike concentrated on the crippled *Zuiho* and she soon went under. The last two attacks of the day inflicted little damage on the fleeing Japanese, but TF38 had already sunk three carriers and damaged a fourth. Halsey was pounding along Ozawa's wake with the hope of bringing his

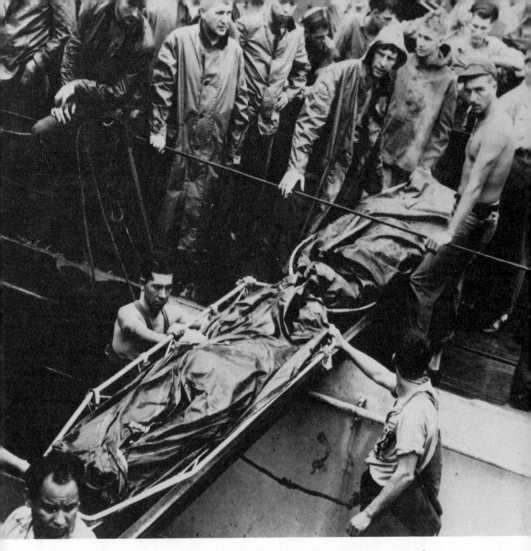

Two of the many Americans killed during the desperate Japanese attacks on the invasion fleet at Leyte Gulf are transferred to another ship.

battleships into range of the survivors. Meanwhile, Kinkaid, some 250 miles to the south, was filling the airwaves with frantic appeals for help against Kurita's fleet.

Admiral Nimitz, anxiously monitoring the situation at Pearl Harbor, sent a message to Halsey, with copies to Admiral King in Washington and to Kinkaid seeking information from Halsey. The communications officer who encoded the message added the usual padding to confuse enemy cryptographers, using the words "the world wonders." When the message was received on board the

On October 25, 1944, a 250-kilogram bomb, dropped by a Japanese kamikaze, sliced between the flight and hangar decks of the escort carrier *Suwannee* and exploded.

Ninety minutes after a kamikaze attack ripped a hole in the flight deck, the crew of the *Suwannee* repaired and patched the deck and the carrier was ready for flight operations.

New Jersey, Halsey's flagship, it was thought the final phrase was part of the message and it was rushed to the Admiral in the following form: "Where is Rpt Where Is Task Force Thirty Four RR The World Wonders."

Halsey was furious when he read the message. "I was stunned as if I had been struck in the face," he wrote later. "The paper rattled in my hands. I snatched off my cap [and] threw it on the deck."[50] Regarding the message as a public slap in the face from Nimitz, he delayed for an hour—saying he was refueling his ships —before reluctantly leading the major elements of the task force south. Ozawa's ships were only 42 miles away, Halsey claimed, and he later declared that the gravest error he had made during the battle was "bowing to pressure and turning south."[51] In any event, it was too late to catch Kurita. Fearing that the Americans had now had time to concentrate their forces against him, he broke off his pursuit of "Taffy 3" and escaped through the San Bernardino Strait.

The battle was not over yet, however. Although he had taken most of his fleet south with him, Halsey had sent a force of cruisers and destroyers in pursuit of Ozawa's cripples. They sank the *Chiyoda,* the remaining Japanese carrier, and a destroyer before the chase was called off. The final blows of the day were delivered by the kamikazes, who made their first appearance after Kurita had beaten a retreat. "Taffy 1," the southernmost of the escort carrier groups, sustained the first attack when a Zero crashed into the *Santee,* setting her afire. The flames had just been extinguished when she was struck by a torpedo fired by a Japanese submarine, but she survived—a remarkable tribute to her design and her crew. The *Suwannee* also survived a direct hit, but the *St. Lo,* of "Taffy 3," was not so lucky. She was struck by a suicide plane which crashed through her flight deck, exploding among a store of bombs and torpedoes, making her the first warship to be sunk by a kamikaze.

So ended the Battle for Leyte Gulf—in reality four separate actions fought largely outside that body of water. The Japanese had lost four aircraft carriers, three battleships, nine cruisers and ten destroyers—more tonnage than was lost by both sides at Jutland, the major naval battle of World War I.

Early in 1945 Admiral Spruance relieved Halsey, and once again

A pilot wounded during the Battle of Leyte Gulf is removed from his damaged F6F Hellcat aboard the *Lexington*. The rugged construction of the Hellcat enabled many such pilots to return to their ship, and aided in producing the Hellcats' kill-to-loss ratio of nine to one.

the Third Fleet became the Fifth Fleet. Roaming at will, the sixteen fast carriers of TF58 established an arc of destruction about Japan that reached from Okinawa to Formosa. The first stage in the final assault on the home islands was the seizure by the Marines of Iwo Jima. This small island, midway between Saipan and Tokyo, was to be used by fighters accompanying the American B-29 bombers that were leveling Japanese cities. To prevent enemy interference, Admiral Mitscher launched an attack on the airfields near Tokyo in which some 340 Japanese planes were shot down and another 190 were destroyed on the ground.

Meanwhile, the Royal Navy had gone on the offensive in the Indian Ocean. Victory in the Mediterranean and the end of the threat posed by the *Tirpitz* permitted the Admiralty to send the

Illustrious and *Victorious*, and later the *Indomitable*, to join the Eastern Fleet. Flying off a mixture of British- and American-built planes, they raided targets in the Bay of Bengal and the East Indies, and provided diversions for American operations in the Pacific. The *Saratoga* briefly joined them for an attack on the harbor of Sabang Island off the northern tip of Sumatra, and on the oil refinery at Surabaya on Java. During the invasion of the Philippines, the *Indomitable* and *Victorious*, accompanied by a battle cruiser, four cruisers, and ten destroyers, made repeated strikes against Nicobar Island in the Bay of Bengal—the first sustained operation conducted by the British carriers.

Roosevelt and Churchill had agreed in September 1944 that the British fleet should take part in operations in the Pacific. The latter part of that year was spent in re-equipping the carriers and re-training the crews so that their operations would mesh with the Americans'. The British Pacific Fleet, as it was now designated, was placed under the overall command of Admiral Sir Bruce Fraser, and its Carrier Squadron, which totaled four ships after the arrival of the *Indefatigable*, was commanded by Vice-Admiral Sir Philip Vian, who had commanded the escort carriers off Salerno. This force included some 240 aircraft—a few Seafires and

The light carrier *Monterey* rests at anchor at Ulithi following the Battle of Leyte Gulf and operations in the Philippine Sea. An *Independence*-class carrier, the *Monterey* displaced 11,000 tons and carried 45 aircraft.

Fireflies, but mostly Hellcats, Avengers, and Corsairs. In fact, the British had more success than the Americans in using the Corsair as a shipboard fighter.

In January 1945, the Royal Navy moved its base from Trincomalee, Ceylon—called "Scapa Flow in Technicolor" by British sailors —to Sydney, Australia. On the way, Vian launched a massive strike against the oil refineries at Palembang, in southern Sumatra, source of much of Japan's aviation fuel. Forty-three Avengers, a dozen rocket-firing Fireflies and about fifty fighters raided the Soengi Gerong refinery on January 24, destroying most of the

On November 5, 1944, American aircraft from the eleven carriers of Task Force 38 of Admiral Halsey's Third Fleet struck Japanese-occupied Luzon in the Philippines. The Americans lost 25 planes, but destroyed over 400 enemy aircraft and sank the heavy cruiser *Nachi* in Manila Bay. She had collided with the *Mogami* during the Battle of Leyte Gulf in October, but managed to return to Manila for repairs which were not completed on November 5 when, hastily maneuvering about five miles from Corregidor, she was bombed by warplanes from the *Lexington* and sank, stern first.

After the seizure of the Philippines, most of the American fast carrier task forces were forward deployed in the Western Pacific; Ulithi was a major fleet anchorage. On February 15, 1945, a Japanese kamikaze penetrated the air defense of Ulithi and crashed into the deck of the fleet carrier *Randolph*, which was at anchor. The gaping hole at the end of the flight deck was so serious that, earlier in the war, the carrier would have had to return home for repairs. By 1945, however, even some of the most serious damage could be repaired by ingenious floating repair ships, one of which came alongside the *Randolph* and patched her up.

Kamikazes preferred to attack American capital ships like the fast carrier *Hancock*, which was struck on November 25, 1944. The suicide plane dived on the carrier from out of the sun but antiaircraft fire destroyed the attacker only 300 feet from the ship. Nonetheless, a wing and fuselage section from the Japanese aircraft landed on the deck of the *Hancock*, engulfing one-half of the vessel in flames and smoke. However, damage control parties quickly put out the fires with only minor damage to the flight deck and the carrier resumed flight operations shortly thereafter.

The spare fuel tanks of an American F6F fighter could be dropped to give the aircraft greater range. However, the belly tank sometimes detached upon landing, as in this incident aboard the *Lexington* in the Pacific on February 25, 1945. The pilot escaped by climbing across the wing and jumping onto the deck.

storage tanks and reducing output by half. Fourteen Japanese planes were shot down, and thirty-four were destroyed on the ground. An attack on the Pladjoe refinery five days later was even more devastating, with the refinery being completely knocked out, and nearly seventy enemy planes destroyed.

Following the capture of Iwo Jima after bloody fighting, an Army-Marine force that eventually totaled more than 200,000 men was landed at Okinawa on Easter Sunday, April 1, 1945. Part of the Ryukyu chain, the island was only 350 miles from Kyushu. The landing was carried out with little Japanese opposition, but the 100,000-man garrison soon made it clear that every foot of the island would be contested. During the softening-up process before the invasion, American carriers and those of British Pacific Fleet, now desigated as TF57, pounded the Japanese airfields on Kyushu, claiming to have destroyed some 500 planes. The *Wasp*, *Enterprise*, *Yorktown* and *Franklin* were all damaged by conventional bombers during this operation—the *Franklin* worst of all. Two bombs ignited planes that were fueled and armed on her flight deck. Ripped by a long series of explosions, the carrier was

On January 12, 1945, American Avenger aircraft of Air Group 4 from the fast carrier *Essex* formed up and flew off to bomb and torpedo airfields and shipping near Saigon in Japanese-occupied Indochina.

saved only through the superhuman efforts of her officers and crew. Even so, 724 men were killed and another 265 were wounded. None of these setbacks interfered with the invasion timetable, however.

Unlike the naval forces at Guadalcanal, where the Marines were abandoned on the beaches, the Fifth Fleet had come to stay—and it remained off Okinawa despite the most concentrated attack ever sustained by any naval force. Beginning on April 6-7, the Japanese launched massive kamikaze attacks, sending 355 planes to crash into the Allied ships and an equal number on conventional bombing runs. Combat air patrols and concentrated antiaircraft fire brought down large numbers of these planes, but some of the kamikazes got through. Hardest hit were the destroyers and supporting ships on radar picket duty around the island, although some of the kamikazes tried to hit the transports and fire-support ships closer to the beachheads. In all, nineteen ships were damaged in this attack, some of them seriously.

During an air raid on the Japanese Yontan Air Field on Okinawa on April 16, 1945, antiaircraft tracers silhouetted American Marine F4U Corsair fighters. This attack took place two weeks after the invasion began, an operation which was scheduled to last one month and which was not completed until June 22.

An American TBM-1C Avenger ascending from the *Yorktown*, enroute to Saigon in January 1945. The TBM was a General Motors version of the Avenger that gradually replaced the TBF built by Grumman. More than 7,000 Avengers of both types were built during World War II.

The Japanese did not confine their suicide attacks to aircraft. The *Yamato* was thrown into the battle on a one-way death ride in which she was to annihilate the invasion fleet with her 18-inch guns. Mitscher's planes sighted the battleship in the East China Sea on the morning of April 7, and he launched a 280-plane strike. The *Yamato* threw up a curtain of antiaircraft fire, but wave after wave of torpedo planes and bombers bored in to the attack. Hit by ten torpedoes and five bombs, the *Yamato* rolled over and sank two hours after the battle had begun. Only 269 men of her crew of nearly 2,500 survived. A light cruiser and four destroyers that had been accompanying the battleship were also sunk. Only ten planes were lost in the attack.

All through April and May, the Allied fleet was subjected to repeated mass kamikaze attacks, as well as raids by conventional bombers. No carriers were lost but Mitscher's flagship, the *Bunker*

201

Hill, was hit by two suicide planes in quick succession and lost 396 men. The Admiral transferred his flag to the *Enterprise,* only to have her also hit by a kamikaze. "Any more of this and there will be hair growing on this old bald head," said Mitscher and he shifted to the *Randolph.* The *Formidable, Victorious* and *Indomitable* were also hit by suicide planes but, unlike the American flat-tops, sustained only minor damage because of their armored flight decks and stout construction. "When a kamikaze hits a U.S. carrier, it's six months' repair in Pearl," observed an American liaison officer. "In a Limey carrier, it's 'Sweepers, man your brooms.' "[52] Round-the-clock pounding of the airfields from which the kamikazes flew, heavy and sustained losses, and a shortage of volunteers and fuel finally brought about a steady reduction in the tempo of attacks. On July 2, the campaign for Okinawa was officially declared completed. In all, the U.S. Navy had lost 34 ships, and 368 were damaged. More than 4,900 sailors were dead or missing and another 4,800 had been wounded.

Impotent at sea and in the air, there was little the Japanese could do, as American and British carrier planes and Army B-29s ranged over the home islands at will. Pursuing the Imperial Navy to its last refuges on the Inland Sea they sank the few remaining battleships and carriers. They were raking airfields and striking at rail yards and other vital facilities in preparation for an invasion of Japan when the atomic bombs over Hiroshima and Nagasaki,

The flight deck of the light carrier *Langley* under repair after being hit by a kamikaze off Formosa, January 21, 1945.

The American escort *Sangamon* was severely damaged by a Japanese kamikaze while covering operations off the coast of Okinawa in May 1945.

along with the entry of the Soviet Union into the war, convinced
the Japanese of the futility of continued resistance.

The formal surrender ceremony took place on Sunday, September 2, 1945 on the battleship *Missouri*, whose massive bulk, surrounded by hundreds of naval vessels, loomed out of the overcast
that cloaked Tokyo Bay. But the Allied aircraft carriers which had
played a key role in bringing the once-proud Japanese Empire to

In the last year of the war, the U.S. Army wanted to seize the Philippines, while the Navy hoped to jump from the Marianas to the Japanese air base on Formosa. In the absence of sufficient service troops to seize Formosa, Admiral King chose Okinawa instead. The Japanese had dug into the rocky soil and caves of the island, and Marine Corsairs had to be sent against these ridge-ringed redoubts to blow out the enemy with rocket barrages.

All belligerents in World War II developed bizarre "super-weapons" to turn the tide. Dropped from high altitude by a Betty bomber, the Japanese "Baka" ("fool") flying bomb carried its 2,645-pound warhead at rocket-assisted speeds of up to 620 mph. This "Baka" was captured by the Americans on Okinawa.

In April 1945, the super-battleship *Yamato*—which featured mammoth 18-inch guns—sortied into the East China Sea on a one-way suicide mission to contest the American invasion of Okinawa. Smothered by over four hundred combatant aircraft from the U. S. Pacific Fleet, the *Yamato*, the light cruiser *Yakagi*, and four escorting destroyers were sunk in the action.

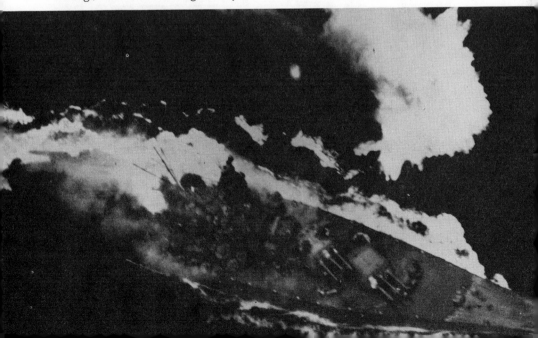

Near the end of the war, in July 1945, the danger from the fanatical kami-kazes was intensified. Already afire from antiaircraft fire from an American warship, this suicide plane attempted to dive on the ship, but missed its objective completely and fell into the Pacific Ocean.

While the carrier *Bunker Hill*—her deck jammed with planes ready to take off—was operating with a fast carrier task force in the "slot" between Okinawa and Kyushu, two Japanese kamikazes struck the ship within thirty seconds of one another. The carrier was saved due to heroic damage control measures, but she had to return to the United States for repairs.

Peace. The small escort carrier *Lunga Point* ploughed through heavy seas on October 6, 1945, off Japan.

its knees rode over the horizon. They had been kept at sea, on Halsey's orders, so they could launch aircraft, in case the Japanese surrender turned out to be a sham. Stern ranks of Allied officers silently greeted the Japanese as they arrived on the battleship, eleven impassive figures in black morning coats or military drab.

"We are gathered here, representatives of the major warring powers to conclude a solemn agreement whereby peace may be restored," intoned General MacArthur. He was stiffly erect but close observers noted his hands were trembling. He called upon the nations of the world to rise above past hatreds "to the higher dignity which alone benefits the sacred purposes we are about to serve." Then, in profound silence, the signing of the surrender terms began, the defeated going first. Having added his own signature to the document and declared the proceedings closed, MacArthur walked over to Admiral Halsey, who had led the Allied fast carriers to Tokyo Bay, and putting his arm around his shoulders, said, "Start 'em now!"

"Aye, Aye, sir!" replied Halsey with a broad smile.

There was a rumbling in the sky and the deck below them trembled as a mass flight of hundreds of carrier planes swept in over the *Missouri* at little more than mast-height. All the great names evocative of aerial combat over the sea were there . . . Hellcats . . . Corsairs . . . Avengers . . . Helldivers . . . their wings seeming to reach from horizon to horizon. Making a long, sweeping turn over the fleet, they flew away into the mist shrouding the snow-crowned tip of Mt. Fuji.

Action Report

Six years in the crucible of war had transformed the aircraft carrier from an untried and somewhat suspect weapon into the dominant force of naval operations. Versatile and flexible, Allied carriers played a vital role in battering the Axis into submission. They attacked battle fleets, escorted convoys, hunted down submarines and surface raiders, ferried aircraft to hard-pressed land bases, and furnished cover for assaults on enemy territory in every theatre of operations. Of course, the air navy had not won the war singlehandedly. The Allied armies, the strategic bomber, the submarine, and the miracle of mass production performed by American workers all contributed to the triumph. But without an Allied victory in the naval air war, the conflict would have lasted far longer and the casualties would have been even more severe.

In the European theatre, the Royal Navy's carriers and the Fleet Air Arm helped keep the supply line to Britain open, maintained Allied control of the Mediterranean, and facing abominable weather conditions and a determined enemy, ensured delivery of the tools of war to the Soviet Union. The naval air war reached its zenith in the Pacific, where the carrier was the cutting edge of both the Japanese and Allied offensives. A Japanese carrier task force knocked out the battleships of the U.S. Navy's Pacific Fleet at Pearl Harbor, inadvertently providing a model for the Fast Carrier Task Force that helped bring Japan to her knees. Carrierborne aircraft halted the Japanese expansion at the battles of Coral Sea and Midway, and then led the advance across the Pacific to the home islands. With a mobility never before seen in naval warfare, the fast carriers brought the "front" ever closer to Japan, and along with the submarine force severed her communications with her newly won empire.

Although the carriers did not mount a massive offensive against Japanese shipping until mid-1944, they accounted for 18 percent of the total tonnage sent to the bottom—second only to the submarines, which sank 54 percent. Interdiction of the oil, coal, raw materials and food that had prompted the Japanese to gamble on war, had ensured their defeat, long before the atomic bombs were dropped on Hiroshima and Nagasaki, and the Russians entered the war. Carrier aircraft also sank a greater proportion of Japan's combat fleet, including five battleships and ten carriers, than any other weapons system.

The far-ranging activities of the Fast Carrier Task Force powerfully refuted the contention of air-power enthusiasts that the bomber had made navies obsolete. "Superior air power will dominate all sea areas when they act from land bases," General "Billy" Mitchell had declared. "No seacraft, whether carrying aircraft or not, is able to contest their aerial supremacy." Wartime experience clearly showed, however, that given adequate fighter protection, carriers could indeed operate successfully within range of shore-based aircraft.

As Admiral Sir Arthur Hezlet has pointed out, the airplane did not render sea power irrelevant. Instead the airplane and the carrier replaced the big gun and the battleship as the measurement of sea power. "The role of ships became firstly one of carrying air power to sea," he said, "secondly of co-operating with aircraft in the exercise of sea power, and thirdly of exploiting the use of the sea when command of it has been won." Working in close harmony, ships and planes have proven to be an almost unbeatable combination. During the wars in Korea and Vietnam, the air navy again demonstrated the mobility, flexibility and strength that have always been the hallmark of sea power.

Notes

1. Walter Lord, *Day of Infamy* (New York: Henry Holt and Company, 1957) p. 12.
2. Samuel Eliot Morison, *The Rising Sun in the Pacific* (Boston, Little, Brown and Company, 1954) pp. 94–95.
3. Masatake Okumiya, Jiro Hirikoshi and Martin Caidin, *Zero!* (New York: Ballantine Books, 1957) pp. 48–49.
4. Mitsuo Fuchida and Masatake Okumiya, *Midway: The Battle That Doomed Japan* (Annapolis, Md.: U.S. Naval Institute, 1955) p. 29.
5. Clark G. Reynolds *The Fast Carriers* (New York: McGraw-Hill Book Company, 1968) p. 1.
6. S. W. Roskill, *White Ensign: The British Navy at War* (Annapolis, Md.: U.S. Naval Institute, 1963) p. 41.
7. Ian Cameron, *Wings of the Morning* (New York: William Morrow, 1963) p. 34.
8. S. W. Roskill, *The War at Sea* (London: Her Majesty's Stationery Office, 1965) Vol. 1, p. 196.
9. Cameron, *op. cit.*, p. 49.
10. *Ibid.*, p. 53.
11. Ludovic Kennedy, *Pursuit* (New York: Viking Press, 1974) p. 119.
12. *Ibid.*, pp. 153–154.
13. John Winton, *Air Power at Sea* (New York: Thomas Y. Crowell, 1976) p. 82.
14. Winston S. Churchill, *Memoirs of the Second World War* (Boston: Houghton Mifflin, 1959) pp. 510–511.
15. Okumiya, Hirikoshi and Caidin, *op. cit.*, p. 68.
16. *Ibid.*, p. 70.
17. *Ibid.*, pp. 76–77.
18. *Ibid.*, p. 79.
19. Morison, *op. cit.* pp. 362–363.
20. Okumiya, Hirikoshi and Caidin, *op. cit.*, p. 92.
21. John B. Lundstrom, *The First South Pacific Campaign* (Annapolis, Md.: U.S. Naval Institute, 1976), unnumbered page.
22. William F. Halsey and Joseph Bryan III, *Admiral Halsey's Story* (New York: Whittlesey House, 1947) p. 103.
23. Walter Lord, *Incredible Victory* (New York: Harper & Row, 1967) p. 3.
24. *Ibid.*, p. 66.
25. *Ibid.*, p. 86.
26. Clarence E. Dickinson and Boyden Sparks, "The Target Was Utterly Satisfying," in *The United States Navy in World War II*, S. E. Smith, ed., (New York: William Morrow, 1966) p. 280.

27. Lord, *Victory,* op. cit., p. 196.

28. Samuel Eliot Morison, *Coral Sea, Midway and Submarine Actions* (Boston: Little, Brown and Company, 1950) p. 138.

29. Okumiya, Hirikoshi and Caidin, *op. cit.* p. 138.

30. Richard Newcomb, *Savo* (New York: Holt, Rinehart and Winston, 1961) p. 172.

31. Samuel Eliot Morison, *The Struggle for Guadalcanal* (Boston: Little, Brown and Company, 1960) p. 105.

32. E. B. Potter, *Nimitz* (Annapolis, Md.: U.S. Naval Institute, 1976) p. 195.

33. *Ibid.,* p. 198.

34. John Deane Potter, *Fiasco* (New York: Stein and Day, 1970) p. 110.

35. Robert Jackson, *Strike from the Sea* (London: Arthur Barker, 1970) p. 110.

36. Hugh Popham, *Sea Flight* (London: William Kimber, 1954) p. 128.

37. Samuel Eliot Morison, *Operations in North African Waters* (Boston: Little, Brown and Company, 1947) p. 163.

38. Karl Dönitz, *Memoirs* (Westport, Conn.: Greenwood Press, 1976) p. 330.

39. Ludovic Kennedy, *Menace: The Life and Death of the Tirpitz* (London: Sidgwick & Jackson, 1979) p. 144.

40. Theodore Roscoe, *On the Seas and in the Air* (New York: Hawthorne Books, 1970) p. 400.

41. C.A.F. Sprague and Philip H. Gustafson, "They Had Us On the Ropes," in Smith, *op. cit,* p. 874.

42. Norman Polmar, *Aircraft Carriers* (Garden City, N.Y.: Doubleday & Co., 1969) p. 380.

43. Roscoe, *op. cit.,* p. 438.

44. *Ibid.,* p. 431.

45. Samuel Eliot Morison, *Leyte* (Boston: Little, Brown and Company, 1958, p. 181.

46. Halsey, *op. cit.,* p. 217.

47. Morison, Leyte, *op. cit.,* p. 253.

48. *Ibid.*

49. Sprague, *op. cit.,* p. 869.

50. Halsey, *op. cit.,* p. 220.

51. Halsey's Notes to Hanson W. Baldwin, "The Shō Plan—the Battle for Leyte Gulf" in *Sea Fights and Shipwrecks* (Garden City, N.Y.: Hanover House, 1955) p. 181.

52. John Winton, *The Forgotten Fleet* (New York: Coward-McCann, 1967) p. 122.

Bibliography

Baldwin, Hanson, *Sea Fights and Shipwrecks* (Garden City, N.Y.: Hanover House, 1955)

Barker, A. J., *Pearl Harbor* (New York: Ballantine Books, 1969)

Belote, James H. and Belote, William M., *Titans of the Sea* (New York: Harper & Row, 1975)

———, *Typhoon of Steel* (New York: Harper & Row, 1970)

Bennett, Geoffrey, *Naval Battles of World War II* (New York: David McKay, 1975)

Bragadin, M.A., *The Italian Navy in World War II* (Annapolis, Md.: U.S. Naval Institute, 1957)

Brown, David, *Carrier Operations in World War II* (Annapolis, Md.: U.S. Naval Institute, 1968–74) 2 vols.

Buell, Thomas B., *The Quiet Warrior* (Boston: Little, Brown, 1974)

Cameron, Ian, *Wings of the Morning* (New York: William Morrow, 1963)

Churchill, Winston S., *Memoirs of the Second World War* (Boston: Houghton Mifflin, 1959)

Dickens, Peter, *Narvik* (Annapolis, Md.: U.S. Naval Institute, 1974)

Dönitz, Karl, *Memoirs* (Westport, Conn.: Greenwood Press, 1976)

Dull, Paul S., *A Battle History of the Imperial Japanese Navy* (Annapolis, Md.: U.S. Naval Institute, 1978)

Field, James A., *The Japanese at Leyte Gulf* (Princeton: Princeton University Press, 1947)

Fuchida, Mitsuo and Okumiya, Masatake, *Midway: The Battle That Doomed Japan* (Annapolis, Md.: U.S. Naval Institute, 1953)

Grenfell, Russell, *The Bismarck Episode* (New York: Macmillan, 1962)

———, *Main Fleet to Singapore* (London: Faber and Faber, 1951)

Griffith, Samuel B., II, *The Battle for Guadalcanal* (Annapolis, Md.: The Nautical and Aviation Publishing Co. of America, 1979)

Halsey, William F. and Bryan, Joseph, *Admiral Halsey's Story* (New York: Whittlesey House, 1947)

Hezlet, Sir Arthur, *Aircraft and Sea Power* (New York: Stein & Day, 1970)

Irving, David, *The Destruction of Convoy P.Q. 17* (London: Cassell, 1968)

Jackson, Robert, *Strike From the Sea* (London: Arthur Barker, 1970)

Kennedy, Ludovic, *Menace: The Life and Death of the Tirpitz* (London: Sidgwick & Jackson, 1979)

———, *Pursuit* (New York: Viking Press, 1974)

Lord, Walter, *Day of Infamy* (New York: Henry Holt, 1957)

———, *Incredible Victory* (New York: Harper & Row, 1967)

Lundstrom, John B., *The First South Pacific Campaign* (Annapolis, Md.: U.S. Naval Institute, 1976)

213

Macintyre, Donald, *The Naval War Against Hitler* (New York: Charles Scribner's Sons, 1971)

Middlebrook, Martin and Mahoney, Patrick, *Battleship: The Loss of the Prince of Wales and the Repulse* (London: Penguin Books, 1979)

Miller, Nathan, *The U.S. Navy: An Illustrated History* (Annapolis, Md.: U.S. Naval Institute, 1977)

Millot, Bernard, *The Battle of the Coral Sea* (Annapolis, Md.: U.S. Naval Institute, 1974)

Morison, Samuel Eliot, *History of United States Naval Operations in World War II* (Boston: Little, Brown, 1947–62) 15 vols.

Newcomb, Richard F., *Savo* (New York: Holt, Rinehart and Winston, 1961)

Okumiya, Masatake and Jiro Hirikoshi with Martin Caiden, *Zero!* (New York: Ballantine Books, 1957)

Polmar, Norman, *Aircraft Carriers* (Garden City, N.Y.: Doubleday & Co., 1969)

Popham, Hugh, *Sea Flight* (London: William Kimber, 1954)

Potter, E. B., *Nimitz* (Annapolis, Md.: U.S. Naval Institute, 1976)

Potter, John Deane, *Fiasco* (New York: Stein & Day, 1970)

Reynolds, Clark G., *The Fast Carriers* (New York: McGraw-Hill, 1968)

Roscoe, Theodore, *On the Seas and in the Skies* (New York: Hawthorne Books, 1970)

Roskill, S. W., *The War at Sea* (London: Her Majesty's Stationery Office, 1956–61) 3 vols.

———, *White Ensign: The British Navy at War* (Annapolis, Md.: U.S. Naval Institute, 1960)

Ruge, Friedrich, *Der Seekrieg: The German Navy's Story 1939–1945* (Annapolis, Md.: U.S. Naval Institute, 1957)

———, *The Soviets as Naval Opponents: 1941–45* (Annapolis, Md.: U.S. Naval Institute, 1979)

Sherrod, Robert, *History of Marine Corps Aviation in World War II* (Washington: Combat Forces Press, 1952)

Smith, S. E., ed., *The United States Navy in World War II* (New York: William Morrow, 1966)

Stafford, Edward P., *The Big E* (New York: Random House, 1962)

Taylor, Theodore, *The Magnificent Mitscher* (New York: W. W. Norton, 1954)

Tillman, Barrett, *The Dauntless Dive Bomber in World War Two* (Annapolis, Md.: U.S. Naval Institute, 1976)

Tute, Warren, *The Deadly Stroke* (New York: Coward, McCann & Geoghegan, 1973)

United States Strategic Bombing Survey, *The Campaigns of the Pacific War* (New York: Greenwood Publishers, 1970)

Van Oosten, F. C., *The Battle of the Java Sea* (Annapolis, Md.: U.S. Naval Institute, 1976)

Winton, John, *Air Power at Sea* (New York: Crowell, 1976)

———, *The Forgotten Fleet* (New York: Coward-McCann, 1967)

Woodward, C. Vann, *The Battle for Leyte Gulf* (New York: Macmillan, 1947)

Photos

Photographs on the following pages are reproduced courtesy of Popperfoto: pages 12, 13, 17, 18, 20, 22(t), 24, 28(t), 31(t), 32, 34(t), 34(b), 36, 49(t), 49(b), 50, 51, 52, 64, 82, 84, 143, 144, 149(b), 163, 185, 189, 196, 197, 198(t), 198(b), 204, 205(b), 206, 207.

Photographs on the following pages are reproduced courtesy of the British Imperial War Museum: pages 22(b), 53, 65(t), 65(b), 123, 124, 129, 149(t).

All other photographs are official U.S. Government photos.

Page 2. The *Shaw* explodes during the Japanese attack on Pearl Harbor, December 7, 1941.

Page 14. A squadron of Swordfish in flight.

Page 26. Spitfires warm up on the flight deck of a British carrier.

Page 42. Allied convoy underway for Murmansk, early July 1942.

Page 54. Japanese Nakajima G3M2 Nell bombers flying a mission against Bataan, 1942.

Page 68. The *Lexington* burning at the Battle of the Coral Sea.

Page 98. A Japanese bomb splashes astern a U.S. carrier at the Battle of the Santa Cruz Islands, October 16, 1942.

Page 120. The German battleship *Gneisenau.*

Page 152. TBMs, SBDs, and F6Fs on the flight deck of the *Lexington* during strikes on Saipan.

Page 176. A Japanese twin-engine bomber misses a U.S. carrier in action west of the Marianas, June 1944.

Index

All page numbers italicized indicate photographs or captions.

INDEX

222

Library of Congress Cataloging in Publication Data

Miller, Nathan, 1927-
  The naval air war, 1939-1945.

  Bibliography: p.
  Includes index.
  1. World War, 1939-1945--Naval operations.
2. World War, 1939-1945--Aerial operations.
3. World War, 1939-1949--Pacific Ocean. I. Title.
D770.M48   940.54'4   79-90171
ISBN 0-932852-11-8